THE
ORIGINS OF CHRISTIAN
SUPERNATURALISM

THE
ORIGINS OF CHRISTIAN
SUPERNATURALISM

BY

SHIRLEY JACKSON CASE

THE UNIVERSITY OF CHICAGO PRESS

CHICAGO · ILLINOIS

BX 751
C330

The University of Chicago Press · Chicago 37
Agent: Cambridge University Press · London

PREFACE

IN RECENT years there has been a vigorous revival of interest in supernaturalism. It is often assumed that Christianity introduced this way of thinking into the ancient world and that it thus became the specifically accrediting item in the new religion. Hence one may feel that the reassertion of supernaturalism today is necessary in order to maintain the uniqueness of Christianity. The present volume has been written to clarify opinion on this subject.

Interest in the supernatural was not at all a unique feature of primitive Christianity. At the outset its various rivals abounded in supernatural imagery. This was the common language employed in that day by many different cults to justify their religious practices and traditions. In order to prove its superiority, Christianity had to adopt and heighten this popular language. Only thus could it show itself to be more fully equipped with divine credentials than were any of its predecessors. It met them on their own ground and surpassed them all by magnifying a standard of excellence with which they were already familiar.

When the origins of Christian supernaturalism are viewed in the light of the local conditions that determined its rise and development, the provisional character of this mode of interpretation becomes apparent. The original genius of Christianity as a moral and spiritual way of life is seen to have been gradually overlaid with a veneer of otherworldly imagery that obscured the fundamental nature of the new religion.

The decorative garment in which it was clothed to please the
eye of a miracle-loving age took precedence over the essential
body of religious ideals that inspired worthy Christian living.
A hypothetical form of religious belief was made to antedate
and condition the practical realization of a virtuous religious
life.

The present volume presents a survey of historical data
previously used in my *Experience with the Supernatural in
Early Christian Times,* published in 1929 and long since out
of print. The pertinence of the subject today seemed to demand a review of the whole field with more specific reference
to the problem of origins.

SHIRLEY JACKSON CASE

FLORIDA SCHOOL OF RELIGION
LAKELAND, FLORIDA

CONTENTS

CHAPTER I

SUPERNATURALISM IN THE ANCIENT WORLD

THE sky hung low in the ancient world. Traffic was heavy on the highway between heaven and earth. Gods and spirits thickly populated the upper air, where they stood in readiness to intervene at any moment in the affairs of mortals. And demonic powers, emerging from the lower world or resident in remote corners of the earth, were a constant menace to human welfare. All nature was alive—alive with supernatural forces.

Supernatural agents were active in every area of man's experience. They guided the sun and the moon and the stars in their course across the heavens. Thunder and lightning were their playthings. By their control of the rain clouds they blest the earth with fruitful showers or deluged it with floods and parched it with drought. They caused the eruption of angry volcanoes, and they shook the world with violent earthquakes. They let raging storms loose upon land and sea. They gave fertility to the soil, or they withheld its fruits and afflicted its inhabitants with deadly famine.

The common man lived his life under the constant danger of interference by arbitrary supernatural powers. They might deprive him of his health if he by accident or design incurred their displeasure. He anxiously craved their favor for the simplest forms of his daily conduct. If he proposed to go on

a journey or to engage in a business venture, he first sought
to placate some meddlesome spirit who might be concerned
with his doings. When misfortune or disaster overtook him,
he ascribed it to the inimical activity of some invisible being.

Religion was man's only safeguard in the precarious venture of living. He must discover ways of averting the ill will
of his mysterious foes. Since they were supernatural beings,
the only religion that could be effectively employed for his
protection must itself be supernaturally accredited. Such being the mind of the common man in the world where Christianity arose, this new religion grew in popularity as its
missionaries gradually convinced the peoples of the Roman
Empire that its supernatural credentials surpassed those of its
many rivals.

I

Christianity inherited from Palestinian Judaism an elaborate set of supernatural beliefs. Among Jews, despite their
strong monotheistic leanings, a wide variety of supernatural
powers conditioned the experiences of men. In Palestine the
sky was so near to the earth that angels traversed the inter-
vening space with the utmost ease and in the briefest moment
of time. They hovered between heaven and earth, watching
constantly over the activities of mankind. Similarly, menacing
demons were ever on the alert to snare the unwary and afflict
mortals with sore distress. In fact, the forces of good and evil
were thought to be so much at home on earth that they were
actually engaged in a deadly struggle with each other for the
complete possession of the terrestrial regions. The natural
world, in any modern sense of that term, was totally unknown
to popular Jewish thinking at the beginning of the Christian

Era. By common consent all of life's most treasured experiences, and the solution of its gravest problems, were assigned to the sphere of the supernatural.

The Jews had been much more successful than many of their neighbors in devising a dependable machinery for securing the regular operation of supernatural power on behalf of mankind. They maintained an elaborate system of worship in connection with their temple at Jerusalem, all in accordance with what they believed to be explicit instructions from heaven. Their priests were a special class set apart by God, and their sacrifices were established by divine appointment. The great festive seasons of their religious year were occasions for experiencing anew the presence of the Lord. The weekly gatherings at the synagogue, where the Scriptures were read and expounded, furnished a perpetually repeated opportunity for ascertaining the divine will over a wide range of daily contacts. The entire life of the faithful Jew was supernaturally directed by means of the duly constituted rites of his religion.

Present assurances were heightened by remembrance of the past, when supernatural displays had been more spectacular. In ancient times the normal course of life had been frequently interrupted by unique exhibitions of God's interference in mundane affairs. By a special act he had created the heavens and the earth, he had brought the first human family into being, and he had designed the course of human history. And the evidence of God's interest in earthly happenings was thought to be displayed in a very unusual manner in the history of the Hebrew people. They were the great miracle race.

The supernatural ordering of ancient Hebrew history was amply exhibited in the Scriptures. Here one read that Abraham had been explicitly commanded by God to leave his native land and take up residence in Canaan. There God had watched over his welfare, directing his immediate course of action and sustaining him with promises of success for his descendants. The divine favor had secured for Abraham a line of successors by giving to him and his wife a child in their old age when they were long past the normal period of fruitfulness. And, by instituting the rite of circumcision, God had indicated that henceforth the seed of Abraham should be the chosen race.

At many times in the history of Abraham's descendants heaven was believed to have intervened on their behalf. This was particularly true in periods of special distress such as their days of bondage in Egypt. The waters of the Red Sea and the river Jordan had been miraculously dried up for the Israelites to pass out of Egypt and finally to enter the land of Canaan. While they were still wandering in the wilderness, God had given them for guidance a pillar of cloud by day and a pillar of fire by night. More marvelous still had been the divine favor manifest in the delivery to Moses of the two tables of stone on which God himself had inscribed the Decalogue. When death from thirst threatened the pilgrims in the desert, water was miraculously produced from a rock, or poisonous springs were made sweet, in consequence of God's instructions to Moses. Starvation was averted by the gift of manna from heaven. When the walled city of Jericho blocked entrance into Canaan, God devised a plan for the destruction of its ramparts. The Jew confidently believed that his title to Palestine had been supernaturally guaranteed.

Subsequent periods of history had been continuously directed from heaven. In the days of the Judges, God had been very active in raising up leaders and in supervising their exploits. When the time arrived for the establishment of the monarchy, a miraculously born prophet, Samuel, was at hand to give advice to the nation regarding the choice of its first king. David and his son Solomon had been especially sponsored by God, notwithstanding their manifest human weaknesses. Even when the nation was divided by revolution and threatened with destruction by foreign foes, divine supervision was not wholly lacking. God raised up prophets to be his spokesmen for the guidance of the afflicted people.

In a setting in which all serious thinking about the greatest problems of life moved upon a dominantly supernatural plane it is not surprising that the maintenance of good government should also have been thought the business of deity. When properly constituted, church and state were essentially identical institutions for the Jew. He was never a precocious pupil in the school of practical politics. The more devoted he was to his traditional religion, the more difficult was it for him to reconcile himself to the order of things prevailing in Palestine under a foreign conqueror such as the Romans. To one who was convinced that this territory was a holy land which God had promised by irrevocable covenants to deliver to his chosen people for their perpetual possession, Roman domination seemed clearly to represent a temporary stay of the divine purpose. Some day the depressed nation would be granted redemption.

Although they were thoroughly devoted to supernaturalism, the Jews of Palestine at the beginning of the present era were singularly free from indulgence in magic and other gross displays of superstition that often marked the life of their gentile neighbor. They were spared many of the inconveniences attending the operation of divine agencies in a heathen society in which superhuman forces had not been so well harnessed and so thoroughly subjected to the needs of an organized community. The divine will could now be known by well-established procedures sanctified through custom. The study of Scripture, attendance upon the synagogue services, and the instructions derived from the oral tradition passed on by successive generations of rabbinical scholars served as a normal guide to the will of God. But it would be a grave error to imagine that Jewish religionists in the time of Jesus had any thought of abandoning supernaturalism for what a modern world might call an empirically based attack upon the problems of life and conduct.

The earliest Christians carried over from Judaism a full measure of supernatural beliefs. They entertained the same limited view of the world about them: the floor of heaven was clearly visible in the sky, the lower world was not far from the surface of the earth, God and the angels were ever near in the upper air, Satan and his demons were a constant menace— all these supernatural powers surrounding men every day. It was assumed that all men were inextricably entangled in the meshes of supernaturalism from which there was no escape, but which could be made a great source of comfort and profit for those whose conduct merited the divine approval. Christians even believed that they heightened the significance of this Jewish heritage by the distinctive notes in their preaching. But, failing to win the general approval of their Jewish kinsmen, they turned ultimately to the gentile world.

II

Gentiles looked with high favor upon supernaturalism. Their attachment to this way of thinking was as pronounced as that of the Jews and in some respects was even more extravagant. In the early stages of Greek and Roman culture, mythology had answered all questions regarding the origin of the world and of man. As among the Jews, it was assumed that mankind and human history had been subject to the domination of superhuman powers. The gentile deities were legion, and in accordance with their own desires they played at will with the affairs of men. Escape from their arbitrary power was possible only through assiduous attention to more or less elaborate ceremonies performed to avert their wrath or win their favor. They controlled the fertility of the earth, they were responsible for all meteorological phenomena, pestilence and famine were their instruments, sickness and health depended upon their pleasure, and the whole range of man's experience upon earth was subject to the arbitrary will of supernatural agencies.

There were, however, numerous protests against the vogue of supernaturalism in the Roman world at the beginning of the Christian Era. The Gentiles were far more keenly aware than were the Jews of the rights which naturalism might claim as its own. The work of the ancient Greek physicists had not been completely forgotten, nor did Roman society lack men of intellectual acumen who vigorously protested against the crude superstitions that still abundantly survived in the popular religions.

The rise of Greek philosophy had tended to undermine many popular religious notions. Some philosophers expressed doubt about the very existence of the gods and proposed a purely natural origin for the world and mankind. They also offered a purely naturalistic interpretation of the history of human society free from the activity of any meddlesome divinities or demons. It is very true that not all philosophers were thoroughgoing naturalists, but the tendency of all philosophical thinking was in the direction of reducing the domains of the supernatural.

Among the different philosophical tendencies current in the Roman Empire, Stoicism was one of the most influential. Its advocates made a vigorous attempt to attain a unified view of the world by eliminating the conflict between the natural and the supernatural. But their program actually resulted in the adoption of a denatured supernaturalism by which the area of the natural was virtually supernaturalized. In place of the gods and demons who, according to popular superstition, played freakishly with the affairs of men, the Stoic substituted a sober and well-behaved divine power called the Logos, or divine reason, which was said to pervade all matter and, indeed, to constitute the primal material out of which the entire universe was composed. As a consequence of this essentially pantheistic philosophy the Stoics talked a language which, to the common man at least, left room for a large measure of allegiance to his religious traditions.

Although Stoicism gained wide popularity in the Roman Empire, it never made any serious inroads upon the widespread supernaturalism of the masses. Stoics themselves were very sober in their language when they spoke of gods and divine providence. Later representatives of the school, like Seneca, Epictetus, and Marcus Aurelius, continued to use language which the illiterate man could adopt without essentially altering the imagery of the popular superstition to which he was fondly attached. Indeed, some two hundred years earlier, in Cicero's day, a Stoic philosopher had felt no hesitation in affirming that one might properly regard as manifestations of the divine mind—indeed, as gods—the firmament, the sun, the moon, the world itself, and all things therein useful to mankind. Also, the stories of traditional mythology were not to be rejected outright but were thought capable of reinterpretation by an allegorical process that enabled one to find them all still true if understood in the Stoic way.

The extremes of superstition alone were subjected to a vigorous Stoic criticism. To fear the gods, said Seneca, who are the source of all our good and happiness, is sheer madness on the part of men. No intelligent person would indulge in morbid fancies about the terrors of the future life. There is no prison-house, no lake of fire or river of forgetfulness, no judgment seat, no renewal of the rule of tyrants.[1] Gods are not to be feared but are to be revered, and there is no escape from their presence. The Stoic poet Aratus had said that the godhead of Zeus "fills all streets, all thronging marts of men, the boundless sea and all its parts, whose aid all mortals need, for we are his offspring." And a Christian preacher felt no hesitation in citing this sentiment in support of his own type of supernaturalism (Acts 17:28).

The most uncompromising critics of ancient religious beliefs were the philosophers of the Epicurean school. They declared it to be their great mission in life to deliver their

[1] Seneca *Dial*. vi. 19. 4.

fellow-men from the terrible fear which the popular religion of the day had inspired. Their material universe was a purely natural product of space and atoms. While not refusing to believe in the existence of deities, the Epicureans allowed no place for them in the world of human experience. All dread of the future was removed by denying outright the current notion of the soul's immortality. Also, the gods, themselves composed of material atoms, were relegated to remote parts of the universe where they dwelt in an ideal state of happiness entirely undisturbed by the affairs of mankind. They were entirely free from troubles themselves, and they imposed none on others. So declared the Epicurean spokesman in the early part of Cicero's dialogue on the nature of the gods.

Although Epicureanism had many disciples among the people of the Roman world, it was never the faith of the majority, particularly of the common people. This fact is evident from the statements of the Epicureans themselves. They vigorously protested against what they saw in the society about them, but at the same time they clearly intimated the failure of their skeptical gospel. The language of Lucretius, the well-known Roman exponent of the school in the middle of the first century B.C., is most revealing in this connection. As he looked out on the world about him, he saw the worship of the gods spread over great nations. Towns were filled with altars, and society was given over to the performance of a multitude of sacred rites "now in fashion on solemn occasions and in solemn places, from which even now is implanted in mortals a shuddering which raises new temples of the gods over the whole earth and prompts men to crowd them on festive days."[2]

[2] Lucretius *Nature of Things* v. 1161 ff.

Pliny the Elder, writing from an Epicurean point of view before the year A.D. 79, penned a noteworthy chapter criticizing the prevalent beliefs regarding the deities then in vogue throughout the Roman Empire. His comments are especially significant as indicating the extravagant supernaturalism prevalent at the time. Pliny believed it a sign of human weakness to seek to give shape and form to the deity. If, indeed, there is any god at all, he is "all sense, all sight, all hearing, all life, all spirit and wholly self-contained."[3] This language made its appeal only to the few who, ever since the time of Xenophanes of Colophon in the sixth century B.C., had occasionally affirmed the absurdity of creating gods in man's image. But this was still a widely popular way of making the deities real and vivid to the eyes of mortals.

Pliny thought it still greater folly to pursue a custom of more recent origin, which not only made gods in human shape but created a multitude of divine counterparts for the virtues and vices of men. Conscious of its own infirmity, human nature had made a deity for every experience or emergency that might be encountered in the course of life. Thus innumerable divinities with a variety of names arose, even diseases and plagues being deified in consequence of man's anxiety to propitiate these enemies. When each individual thus makes a separate god for himself, we can readily understand, says Pliny, how it has come to pass that there is even a greater population of the celestials than of human beings.

The custom of worshiping the emperor was less vigorously condemned, but it was given a purely naturalistic interpreta-

---

[3] Pliny *Natural History* ii. 7. 14; cf. Cicero *Laws* ii. 11. 28.

tion. It had originated out of a desire to reward certain individuals for their services to their contemporaries and consequently was a mere honorary gesture due their memories. But Pliny was more offended by the avidity with which many persons in his day were turning for help to foreign and strange cults, especially those that came out of the Orient. It seemed to Pliny that many people were becoming slaves to these intruding rites, and he viewed their conduct with strong disapproval. He says that "they carry on their fingers the gods and the monsters whom they worship, they condemn and they invent various foods, they impose on themselves dreadful ordinances that dispel their quiet sleep; indeed, they neither marry, nor adopt children, nor do anything else without the aid of their sacred rites."

Pliny censured every form of overzealous supernaturalism that was rampant in the gentile world of his day. It seemed to him the *reductio ad absurdum* in religion, but the great masses of the population were of a different opinion. They were enmeshed in the rites of traditional polytheism, or were seeking help from new divinities, and were daily sinking deeper and deeper into the mire of gross superstition from which Epicurean skepticism was unable to deliver them. Preachers of this strenuous gospel of doubt continued for centuries to raise their voices in protest against the ever increasing superstition of their times, but they were always more or less conscious of representing only the minority, and their most serious utterances often betrayed a pathetic note of futility. The message which the aged Diogenes inscribed on the wall of the portico in Oenoanda about the year A.D. 200 is prophetic of the failure that awaited the whole Epicurean cause. Said Diogenes: "If

it were one or two or three or four or five or six or as many as
you like of such, but not too many, who were in evil plight,
I might have visited each individually and tendered them the
best advice as far as in me lay. But the vast majority of men
suffer from the plague of false opinions and the number of
victims increases, for in mutual emulation they catch the contagion from one another like sheep."[4]

Into this gentile world Christianity came as another new
religion out of the Orient, and it won its way not by attacking
supernaturalism but by heightening its significance for its
gentile adherents and extending it to areas of thought and life
more suitable to their needs.

III

The first Christian preachers viewed the religious activities
of the Gentiles with horror and disgust. In the early years of
the missionary enterprise the representatives of Christianity
were men of Jewish heritage and training who shared with
their Palestinian kinsmen a very strong prejudice against
heathenism. It was no novelty for the Christian Paul, brought
up under the tutelage of Judaism, to declare that the use of
material objects to typify the deity was evidence of a senseless
and darkened mind. All the wisdom of Greek philosophy was
of no avail for a people who changed the glory of the incor-
ruptible God into the likeness of a mortal man or represented
him in the form of birds and four-footed beasts and creeping
things (Rom. 1:21–25).

Although sharply condemning gentile idolatry, Christians
had no sympathy with Epicurean skepticism. They were not

[4] *Fragment* ii, col. 3*f* (William).

enemies of supernaturalism but accounted themselves its best friends. They could not follow the Epicureans even in denying to the gentile gods power to interfere with the affairs of men. While Paul spoke rather disdainfully of the "dumb idols" and declared an image to be "nothing," he possessed a very lively sense of the reality of the demons who, in his opinion, were responsible for the idolatrous customs of the heathen (I Cor. 8:4 ff.; 10:20; 12:2). Christians believed the gentile gods to be very active demonic powers and, as such, a serious menace to human welfare. They were the lords of "this present evil age," the "powers of the air," whose leader Satan dominates the lives of those who walk "according to the course of this age" (Gal. 1:4; Eph. 2:2). Successful fortification against their machinations was possible only when one enjoyed protection by the superior supernatural being, the Lord Jesus Christ.

The outright rejection of gentile idolatry was a Jewish attitude carried over by Christians into the Roman world. They taught their followers both the Jewish view of the world and the supernatural interpretation of history depicted in the Old Testament. The account of the beginnings of the earth and of mankind as told in the sacred books of the Jews found full acceptance in the new religion, which represented itself as a further manifestation of the true revelation already given to the Hebrew people in ancient times. Thus Christians appropriated the Jewish Bible in its entirety. And since among Jews these writings were universally revered as the divine authority for everything in their religion, Christians could easily believe that they also possessed in these documents an inexhaustible fund of supernatural wisdom.

The early Christian preachers taught Gentiles even the supernatural interpretation of politics that had been inherited from Judaism. Paul was no more concerned to induce the Thessalonians to turn from idolatry than he was to inculcate in them an attitude of waiting for the coming of the Son of God from heaven to reward believers on the impending day of judgment (I Thess. 1:9–10). Christian missionaries endeavored to persuade their gentile hearers that an ideal order of society would soon be realized through the descent from heaven of a new ruler in the person of the risen Jesus. He would bring to an end all present political authority and establish a new Kingdom of God on earth.

To the supernatural assurances furnished by Scripture, advocates of Christianity added many new displays of heavenly power on behalf of their cause. This expansion of confidence in the divine favor grew as the new religion was compelled to separate itself from the synagogue. The customary operations of an established institution might still serve in large measure the needs of the Jews for divine guidance. But Christians, excommunicated from the synagogue, had to tap new sources of revelation by making a more immediate appeal to the supernatural. They looked directly to God to display his favor on their behalf in new and unusual ways. Palestinian Christians began the process, and it developed rapidly under the stimulus of conditions on gentile soil.

Christian leaders believed themselves to be in possession of unusual miracle-working power. Paul listed miracles and gifts of healings among the proper functions of a Christian community and represented that God himself had ordained this form of activity (I Cor. 12:10, 28–29). Ability to work miracles through the power of the Spirit was convincing evidence of the superior character of the gospel preached by Paul to the Galatian Christians (Gal. 3:1-5). When the genuineness of his claims to apostleship was called in question by his opponents, he affirmed that in truth "the signs of an apostle were wrought among you in all patience by signs and wonders and miracles." In this he could say that he had not fallen behind "the very chiefest apostles." Evidently in Paul's day power to perform miracles was assumed to be an apostolic credential (II Cor. 12:11-12).

When the author of the Book of Acts wrote a history of early Christianity for a gentile reader named Theophilus, the validity of the new religion was defended by an extended appeal to the supernatural. At the first Pentecost after the death of Jesus tongues of fire had fallen upon the reassembled disciples and empowered them to speak many different languages to the promiscuous throng gathered in Jerusalem. Again, at Peter's command a lame man sprang up and walked. When arrested and charged with violating the Old Testament law against magical practices, the disciples were only the more firmly determined to test the supernatural authority of their new faith. They prayed for boldness of speech and continuance of power to perform healing and signs and wonders through the name of Jesus. Their prayer was answered by an earthquake, while they experienced a new sense of inspiration from the Holy Spirit.

The new religion seemed now to have a twofold divine authentication. It carried forward all the prestige of supernaturalism connected with the history of the Hebrews which was now supplemented by new acts of God on behalf of

Christianity. It was now the new Israel equipped with a superior endowment of heavenly power. Although as yet Christians lacked an elaborate institutional organization for safeguarding their more recent supernatural acquisitions, they had full confidence in their future because of God's immediate interest in their welfare. If their organization was so immature that Ananias and Sapphira could attempt to win false credit for generosity, God himself stood ready to smite down the deceivers in their tracks. When supernatural-power was so immediately available for every emergency, it was quite unnecessary to concern one's self with the disciplinary techniques of early church organization.

Throughout its early history Christianity as described in Acts continued to display many miraculous features. The first martyr, Stephen, in the hour of his execution, witnessed a vision of Jesus on the right hand of God in heaven. Presently Saul of Tarsus was halted in his mad career by the voice of Jesus speaking out of heaven to the persecutor on the way to Damascus. In the meantime missionaries in Samaria encountered the sorcerer Simon, himself no mean wonder-worker, but he was overcome with admiration for the "signs and great miracles" wrought by the Christians. The welfare of the recently converted Saul was also insured at Damascus through a preparatory revelation made to Ananias, who was thus divinely instructed to initiate the recently converted persecutor into the new Christian way of life.

Peter, too, in his activities beyond Palestine continued to play the role of miracle-worker. At his word a sick man of Lydda, bedridden for eight years, was restored to health. At Joppa, Peter displayed still greater supernatural powers. So efficacious were his prayers and so powerful was his command that he restored the deceased Tabitha to life even though she had been so long dead that her body had been prepared for burial. When a broader outlook upon his missionary task was needed, again heaven came to Peter's assistance. In a vision he beheld a vessel containing all manner of beasts let down from the sky and heard a voice say, "What God has cleansed don't make common." Later, when cast into prison by Herod Agrippa, Peter experienced a miraculous deliverance. God sent an angel to loose the chains of the faithful Christian and to smite the Jewish king with death.

Paul also was depicted as a man full of divine power. When he encountered a representative of Satan in the person of the sorcerer Elymas, immediately the apostle was able to smite the heathen miracle man with blindness. The preaching of Paul and Barnabas in Iconium was said to have been accompanied by "signs and wonders, done by their hands." At Lystra when Paul commanded a lame man to stand on his feet, although the invalid had been a cripple all his life, immediately he leaped up and walked. The expansion of the missionary enterprise from Asia to Europe was sponsored by a heavenly vision to which Paul responded, and in this new territory Christian and heathen supernaturalism were immediately pitted against one another. But Paul demonstrated the superiority of the former by commanding the demon to come out of a soothsaying girl at the mention of the name of Jesus. And just as Peter had been miraculously released from the prison of Herod, so Paul and Silas were granted a marvelous deliverance from the jail at Philippi.

Heaven's favor for Paul was especially in evidence during

the shipwreck and subsequent happenings on the way to Rome. Instructed by an angel of God, the apostle was able to cheer his companions and to promise them ultimate safety if they obeyed his commands. When they were cast upon land, Paul's prestige was further enhanced by his complete immunity from the venomous sting of a viper. Normally, when bitten, he ought to have swelled up and fallen down dead immediately, but he shook the creature from his hand into the fire without injury to himself, while the astonished onlookers exclaimed that he was a god.

Supernaturalism rendered its most conspicuous service to Christian history in connection with the story of Jesus' career. The Christian preachers, who felt themselves endowed by heaven to perform wonderful works and who believed the new religion to be especially favored by God, could hardly have avoided crowning their hero Jesus with the halo of miracle. In the several gospels now preserved in the New Testament each writer gave lengthy consideration to the supernatural features of Jesus' person and activity.

Even the oldest gospel, that of Mark, was thoroughly permeated by an interest in the supernatural character of Jesus and his work. At the very outset of his public career he heard a voice from heaven declaring him to be the beloved Son of God. Immediately he entered upon his battle royal with Satan and the evil demons. In the pursuit of his task he raised people from their sickbeds, he restored sight to the blind and power of speech to the dumb, and he gave the palsied ability to walk. He was also superior to all physical forces about him. He could instantaneously multiply a few loaves and fishes until they constituted a superabundance of food for a large multitude. He walked on the sea as easily as upon land, the winds ceased at his rebuke, and all nature obeyed his voice. Even the dead returned to life at his command.

Subsequent gospel writers excelled even Mark in the use of supernaturalism to interpret the career of Jesus. They showed him to be not only a worker of miracles but a distinctly superhuman being in his own person. Accounts of his birth depicted the interest of heaven in his physical generation. He had not been born an ordinary human being, but his mother, having been impregnated by the Holy Spirit, gave birth to the very Son of God. He grew to manhood as a child of heaven, displaying a wisdom superior to that of mortals, and he departed from earth as a divine being whom the powers of the lower world were unable to hold in subjection. Having broken through the gates of Hades, he miraculously returned to show himself to his disciples and in their very presence to rise to heaven.

The institutional growth of Christianity early acquired a full set of supernatural sanctions. To join the church meant not simply a voluntary attachment to a new religious association; it involved also participation in a new type of experience where contact with the divine played an important role. At least among the Gentiles in the time of Paul membership in a Christian society carried with it a feeling of divine renewal entitling the convert to be called "a new creation" in Christ (Gal. 6:15; II Cor. 5:17). Baptism signified, if it did not indeed effect, a union with Christ that was no mere figure of speech but was a very real experience in the emotions and convictions of the disciple. He could now say with confidence that he possessed within himself the presence of Christ, even the very Spirit of God. Christian living meant an actual participation in the life of divinity. On uniting with the church, the natural man gave place to the spiritual man, a supernaturally regenerated person, who was now a veritable sanctuary in which the Spirit of God resided (I Cor. 3:16).

The tendency toward supernaturalism showed itself also in connection with the religious meal of the church. At first it served to remind Jesus' friends of the last supper eaten with him before his crucifixion, and it was repeated in anticipation of the future messianic banquet to be celebrated with his followers when presently he would return in triumph to set up his new kingdom. It was thus that they tried to "proclaim the Lord's death till he come" (I Cor. 11:26). But already in the time of Paul, at least among gentile Christians, a more sacramental feeling had begun to attach itself to the observance. In the Corinthian church drinking the cup of the Lord paralleled drinking the cup of demons (I Cor. 10:21). Just as one was in danger of taking demonic spirits into the body through participation in heathen feasts, so, apparently, it was possible for a Christian to partake of Christ in the sacred elements of the Lord's Supper. In the next century the meal became an actual absorption of the flesh and blood of Christ, a supernatural food that insured immortality for the believer's body. Man's flesh would rise from the grave because it had been nourished on the immortal body and blood of Christ.

In less than a century of historical growth the Christian movement had acquired an elaborate set of supernatural sanctions. It had quite surpassed its original Jewish heritages by the addition of numerous items that more significantly attested its excellence for gentile ways of thinking. It now claimed for itself superiority over all rivals in this domain. Several phases of this development invite further observation.

CHAPTER II
THE VALUE OF APPARITIONS

THOSE ancients who drank deeply at the fountain of supernaturalism placed much confidence in the reality of the spirit world by which they felt themselves surrounded. Gods, angels, demons, and the souls of deceased men seemed accessible to mortal eyes and audible to human ears. Man believed in an otherworldly order of existence because from time to time he met its representatives in his own world. In this area of experience one walked by sight no less than by faith.

A belief in apparitions was fundamental to early Christianity. The appearances of Jesus after his death constituted the most distinctive supernatural credential of the new religion. In the last resort the Christian preacher staked everything upon his conviction that Jesus had been seen in the days following the crucifixion. Paul knew of several such incidents that had occurred even before he himself had his similar experience on the way to Damascus (I Cor. 15:5–8). ⎤

The evidential value ascribed to visions, and particularly to the reappearance of an actual historical person in the weeks following his death, is difficult for the modern man to appreciate. Belief in apparitions is no longer general among educated people. Nowadays one is inclined to smile at ghost stories and to ridicule spiritism. But a very different attitude prevailed in the setting where Christianity arose. The situation of the first Christians can be understood only when one remembers the readiness of people in that ancient world to believe in the reality of visions. The founders of Christianity saw in these supernatural occurrences a supremely valuable evidence of the validity of their cause.

I

In Hebrew tradition the visibility of spirits was an easy inference from the universally accepted belief in the existence of God, hosts of angels, Satan and hordes of demons, and the souls of dead men. In early times apparitions of God himself had been a common occurrence. He visited the Garden of Eden in person to talk with Adam and Eve. On different occasions he conversed with the patriarchs Abraham, Isaac, and Jacob. He also appeared to Moses, and once he entertained four of the leaders of Israel, together with seventy of their elders, at a banquet where they ate in his very presence without any disastrous consequences. At least twice Solomon met God face to face. The prophet Isaiah had received his call to preach directly from the Lord of the universe, and Ezekiel testified that he had looked through the open windows of the heavens and there he beheld visions of God.

In other sections of the Jewish Scriptures there was more hesitation in assuming that the deity ever took on the form of man or met mortals on their own level of reality. To see the face of God was possible only for the angels who dwelt in his presence. No man could have this experience and live. Only when temporarily transported to heaven in a state of ecstasy could the human eye expose itself with safety to the scorching rays emanating from the divine countenance. Exceptions to this rule were rare. While Moses had been so honorable a person that God declared a willingness to talk with him "mouth to mouth," to a prophet he would make himself known only in a vision and would speak to him only in dreams (Num. 12:5–8). Other stories betrayed even greater wariness on the part of both man and God in their approach to each other.

In later Judaism it was believed that God, instead of presenting himself to mankind in human form, was accustomed to show his favor for his people by apparitions of angels or by some unusual display in nature designed to demonstrate unmistakably the presence of divine power in the physical sphere. Supernatural beings of secondary gradation were still free to show themselves to men. Even Satan in the shape of a serpent had visited the Garden of Eden, and from the language of Job one infers that the Adversary was wont to walk manlike to and fro on the earth. But evil spirits designedly kept themselves obscure or masqueraded as angels of light, preferring to carry on their inimical activities among men in as deceptive a fashion as possible. Good spirits were less reserved. While apparitions of God were no longer available, visions of angelic intermediaries became only the more frequent and the more easy of attainment. Thus men knew that divine help was near, and they tested their knowledge by the sight of their eyes.

The Jews made relatively little, however, of human apparitions. They were confident that every individual survived death, but their traditional religious thinking had left the soul of the dead man little or no liberty to wander abroad on earth after the decease of the body. Their ancient Scriptures gave only the faintest intimation that once upon a time the Hebrews may have shared with their neighbors in Canaan a respect for the dead which amounted virtually to deification (I Sam. 28:13; Isa. 8:19). But, by the beginning of the Christian Era, orthodox Jewish thinking employed a very different imagery to picture the state of the dead in Sheol.

The lower world stood ready like a ravenous beast with gaping jaws to gulp down the immortal part of man immediately the spirit was released from the body. A prophet had remarked that Sheol opened its mouth without measure, and a wise man had said that Sheol and Abaddon were never satisfied (Isa. 5:14; Prov. 27:20). Apparently it mattered little what became of the body. When news of Joseph's disappearance was brought to his father Jacob, the bereaved parent immediately assumed that his son was in Sheol, where he would await the father's coming, notwithstanding the fact that Jacob imagined the boy's body had been eaten by wild beasts (Gen. 37:33–35). Similarly, Samuel told Saul that on the morrow he would meet the king and his sons in Sheol, although the prophet with his supernatural knowledge must be assumed to have known beforehand that the bodies of Saul and his sons would the next day be hanging on the walls of Bethshan. Whether a corpse was buried or unburied, the immortal counterpart of the man descended immediately to the lower regions.

In sharp contrast with the ease of entrance into the lower world was the difficulty of exit. No provision was made for an escape. People dwelt there behind firmly secured barriers which in later imagery were watched over by supernatural guardians. Once a spirit passed behind those fast-closed doors, there was no hope of return. David had felt it entirely proper to agonize in prayer for the restoration to health of a sick child; but, once the child had died, David ceased his petitions. Not even God could bring back the spirit that had departed. The only consolation remaining to David was a belief that ultimately he would go to be with the child, but the child could never return to him. In the development of its official religion Judaism barred ever more securely the gates of Sheol.

The desperate situation of the Jewish dead was somewhat relieved in later times by the development of a doctrine of ultimate resurrection. The Scriptures reported teachers in Israel who declared that the oppressed and the slain should be revived, that dead bodies would arise, and that the earth would cast forth the dead and no more cover her slain (Isa. 26:19–21). This hope was certainly a possession of orthodox Jewish piety at the beginning of the Christian Era, but it lent no stimulus to belief in apparitions. Sheol still remained the firmly barred prison-house of spirits until the day of judgment.

In a heathen environment, where dead ancestors were worshiped and where men fondly turned to them for direction in critical moments of life, Jewish teachers had thought to preserve the purity of their religion by pronouncing emphatically against the practice of necromancy. The deuteronomic legislation decreed that the Hebrews, when settled in the Holy Land, should have no one in their midst who was a consulter with a familiar spirit or a wizard or a necromancer (Deut. 18:11). Any man or woman who had a "familiar spirit," which means anyone attempting or claiming ability to consult the spirit of the dead, should be punished with death (Lev. 20:6, 27). In the face of these scriptural injunctions the pious Jew was not disposed to expect or to seek communications from the deceased, nor is it surprising that the followers of Jesus should have incurred hostility from their devout Jewish contemporaries by claiming to have had communications with Jesus after his death (Acts 4:1–7).

Had not the disciples of Jesus been "unlearned and ignorant men" (Acts 4:13)—Galilean peasants and fisherfolk—they might have had more scruples against believing that Jesus had actually appeared to Peter. Possibly they did not at all realize how improbable such an experience would seem to one properly schooled in orthodox Jewish thinking regarding Sheol and the impropriety of indulging in communications with persons who had died. The Christian preachers vainly sought to win any large following from among their Jewish contemporaries who were willing to believe that Jesus had been seen alive again after his crucifixion. That way of thinking was anathema to orthodox Judaism, but a much more congenial atmosphere for the cultivation of this imagery existed in the gentile world.

Indeed, it is not improbable that gentile belief in apparitions ought to be taken more largely into account as a means of explaining how the friends of Jesus themselves had found it possible to attach transforming significance in their own lives to this experience. Already for two centuries or more Palestine had been overrun by conquerors who had brought with them the cultures and popular ways of thinking that were current in the world at large. The pious and educated Jew might successfully guard against these insidious influences from without, but the common man was less well protected.

II

The great popularity of belief in apparitions throughout the whole of the Mediterranean world during the years of Christianity's early history is amply attested by multitudes of stories frequently repeated and widely scattered in both Greek and Roman literature. The fancy of every Greek youth had been nourished on the imagery of Homer, whose poems might be called not only the Bible of the Greeks but also their principal primary and high-school textbook. There one learned in childhood that deceased heroes might reveal themselves to their living friends and that the renowned dead still existed in the lower world where they might on occasion be consulted by the living when a favored individual was permitted to visit the nether regions.

The story of Patroclus' appearance to Achilles to plead with the latter for proper funeral rites must have made a deep impression on the Greek imagination. The spirits of the underworld had refused to accept Patroclus into their fellowship until the usual burial ceremonies had been performed over his body. Thus only could the restless spirit win full release from the flesh. Achilles marveled at the lifelikeness of the apparition and sought to lay hold on it, but it eluded his grasp and disappeared again beneath the earth. Reflecting on this experience, Achilles remarked: "Ah me, there remaineth then even in the House of Hades a spirit and a phantom of the dead, albeit the life be not any wise therein. For all night long hath the spirit of hapless Patroclus stood over me, wailing and moaning, and charged me everything that I should do, and wondrous like his living self it seemed."[1]

[1] *Iliad* xxiii. 64 ff.

Among the Romans the same theme was given classic expression by Vergil. Aeneas on a visit to the lower world met
his father, whose frequent apparitions had induced the son to
undertake the perilous journey to Hades. With tears stream-
ing down his cheeks, Aeneas attempted three times to throw
his arms about his father's neck, but each time the ghostly
substance of the shade proved intangible, for it was "light as
the winds and fleet as the pinions of sleep." Its existence, however, was nonetheless real, even though, like the apparition of
Jesus to Mary Magdalene, it might not be profaned by the
touch of mortal hands.[2]

In popular Roman thinking, ghosts from the infernal regions were constantly breaking through to the upper world to
walk once more on earth. Rites were assiduously observed in
order to quiet these spirits and render them friendly. They
were both feared and reverenced, and there was no means by
which the ghosts could be bound more securely in the lower
world. In fact, the ascent of spirits was made easy by the
opening of the *mundus,* as it was called, a circular pit consecrated to the infernal powers. That ghosts should appear
was taken for granted, and the important matter was to make
sure that they were kindly disposed toward the living. Popular superstition undoubtedly supported the legend reported by
Ovid. Once when the Romans were engrossed in warfare,
they neglected the proper gifts to the *manes,* but with menacing consequences. Many persons were struck dead, and
terrifying apparitions were seen. The tombs having given up
their dead, crowds of ghosts went howling through the
streets of the city and the fields of the countryside.[3]

[2] *Aeneid* vi. 695 ff.; cf. John 20:17.   [3] *Fasti* ii. 549 ff.

Ghostly visitors served many other purposes than merely to secure proper respect for their memories. Sometimes they seem to have shown themselves in order to emphasize the horrible character of certain recent events. Even the Epicurean skepticism of the elder Pliny was not sufficient to restrain him from remarking that the colossal wickedness of the emperor Nero had peopled the dwellings of the Romans with ghosts. Most Romans were more credulous than Pliny and would have been quite ready to accept Christian tradition when told that at the time of Jesus' crucifixion tombs had been opened in the vicinity of Jersualem and that many bodies of the deceased saints had come forth out of the tombs and entered into the city itself, where they showed themselves to many persons.[4]

Not all apparitions were terrifying. Many of them served the interests of genuine affection and loving memory. Children returned to console bereaved parents, the grief of lovers was assuaged by apparitions of prematurely deceased companions, and the longing for communion with departed friends was answered by many a spectral visitation. So numerous were these occurrences in gentile tradition that even a representative selection of illustrations would fill many pages. Certainly persons accustomed to this imagery would find no difficulty, and perhaps much satisfaction, in picturing Jesus appearing after death to his distracted friend Peter, or to his own brother James, or to the faithful women whose devotion and affection sought to express itself by carrying gifts to his tomb.

Among the Christians' gentile contemporaries there were,

---

[4] *Natural History* xxx. 2 (5); cf. Matt. 27:52–53.

it is true, some differences of opinion regarding the possibility of beholding a ghost. While the majority of persons accepted the phenomenon as true beyond all shadow of doubt, among the more educated classes there were some skeptics. Epicureans, for example, who affirmed that the soul had no existence apart from the body, were unable to believe in the reality of ghosts. Nor could gods be seen, since they dwelt far from the abodes of men. On the basis of this philosophy there was no possibility of apparitions either human or divine.

The followers of Plato, while fully believing in the reality both of gods and of disembodied human souls, hesitated to accept popular notions about apparitions. In their opinion the soul was a pre-existent entity not at all dependent for its survival upon union with the body. It was wholly incorporeal in its native state, and, being thus absolutely bodiless, it was lacking in apparitional quality. Only those souls which contained bodily impurities could be seen. The spirit of the man who had given himself over to sin became heavy with an earthly element which rendered it visible and made it desire to cling to this world of sense. Plato had described it as "prowling about tombs and sepulchers in the neighborhood of which one may see certain ghostly apparitions of souls that have not departed pure but are cloyed with sight and are therefore visible."[5]

Men with Stoic leanings found it somewhat easier to believe in the visibility of human spirits. According to their way of thinking, the soul of man was a portion of the divine essence out of which the universe was composed. Hence, whether in the body or out of the body, the soul possessed a real material

[5] *Phaedo* 81D.

existence. It was thus easily conceivable that the soul of the living man might now and then go on a journey to some distant place and return during the hours of sleep. Even after death, so long as the soul maintained its identity, it possessed the quality of visibility. The older Stoics had allowed the soul only a limited period for the enjoyment of personal immortality; ultimately it would lose its identity and be absorbed into the primal divine essence whence it had originally come. Accordingly, apparitions of deceased men were possible at most for only a short time after their death. But later Stoics yielded more completely to the inclinations of the populace and allowed the soul a longer period of independent subsistence.

During the first century of the Christian Era there was a growing disposition, even among the more educated Gentiles, to take seriously belief in apparitions. At the very time when the gospel writers were recording the appearances of Jesus as a means of accrediting their new religion to gentile audiences, literary men among the Greeks and Romans, who hardly knew of Christians, or knew them only to despise their simplicity, were concerning themselves very seriously with the visibility of the spirit world.

Probably Plutarch may fairly be called the best-educated man among the Greeks at the close of the first century A.D. He was widely read in history and philosophy. Being a Platonist in his philosophical leanings, he was a sharp critic of both Epicurean naturalism and popular religious superstitions. But in his opinions regarding the possibility of seeing departed spirits he was among the orthodox. Nor would he concede that he was here indulging himself in a weakness. He believed that the intelligent man had full warrant for such faith. In the second chapter of his life of Dion, whom he placed side by side with the Roman Brutus, he argued for the respectability of spiritism on the ground that if two such men with strong and philosophic minds could have faith in the appearance of specters, there was no reason for moderns to doubt these ancient opinions.

Plutarch's Roman contemporary, the younger Pliny, although more inclined toward Stoic ways of thinking, was also much interested in the question of the reality of ghosts. In a letter to his friend Licinius Sura he asked him whether he believes in the existence of ghosts and whether they have a real form, being a sort of divinity, or are only the visionary impression of a terrified imagination. In support of his own belief that the phenomena are real, Pliny cited the experience of a certain Curtius Rufus who was visited one evening in North Africa by the apparition of an unusually large and beautiful woman. She told him that she was the tutelary power that presided over the territory and predicted the future course of his career, and every detail of the prediction actually came to pass, which seemed to Pliny to attest the genuineness of the apparition.

Perhaps even more convincing for Pliny was the story of Athenodorus' experience in the haunted house at Athens. Athenodorus was a Stoic philosopher who went from Tarsus to Athens, where he noticed the advertisement of a house for rent at a very low price. He learned that prospective tenants were frightened off by a ghost accustomed to haunt the place, but he, being a philosopher, paid no attention to the story. He rented the house, and, when busy with his studies late at night, he suddenly heard the clanking of metal and the rattling of chains. At first he would not admit to himself that he heard these noises, but they grew louder and approached nearer, until finally the ghost entered the very chamber in which Athenodorus was sitting. It beckoned to him to follow it out, which he did after some further persuasion, and, when they entered the courtyard, the specter disappeared. In the morning an excavation made in the courtyard on the spot where the apparition had vanished revealed the chained skeleton of a murdered man, but, when the bones had been collected and publicly burned, the ghost ceased to appear. Evidently the philosopher's doubts about the reality of apparitions must have been completely dispelled.

III

The ancients were familiar not alone with specters from the infernal regions. The heavens also yielded them visions of celestial beings who appeared with an authority and majesty truly divine. While Jewish reserve with reference to apparitions of God was shared by the earliest Christians, the latter possessed in their traditions regarding the appearances of the heavenly Jesus a type of imagery that easily paralleled gentile readiness to believe in visions of an actual divinity. The Christians preached a Jesus who after death had appeared to his disciples and who in their very presence had ascended visibly to heaven. Stephen in the moment of death had seen him standing on the right hand of God in heaven, and he had appeared to Saul, the persecutor, in a blinding blaze of light more brilliant than the noonday sun. For Christians such apparitions of the heavenly Christ were virtually equivalent to the Old Testament imagery of God's own appearing among men. A Christian, perhaps in deference to contemporary Jewish scruples, could affirm that "no man has ever seen God," but immediately he could assert that God has been exhibited to the eyes of men in the person of his only begotten Son. Both in his human form while on earth and in his postresurrection appearances Jesus had made deity visible to human eyes. This way of thinking proved offensive to Jewish sensibilities, as the failure of Christian preaching to Jews amply attested, but such imagery was not at all strange or unwelcome among Gentiles.

Greek tradition was especially rich in suggestions of the visibility of the deity. The whole Greek heritage of literature, sculpture, and painting presented a multitude of divinities, usually in very picturesque fashion, before the eyes of mankind. Gods were accustomed to assume a human form, or some other material semblance, in order to manifest their real presence. Greek legend was rich in stories of occasions when gods had appeared among men to display divine power, to avenge a wrong, or to perform a marvelous deed of kindness. The author of Acts did not think it strange that the people of Lystra should hail Paul and Barnabas as apparitions of Hermes and Zeus. At the time that was a perfectly normal way of thinking for people in that region.

Popular notions about the visibility of the deities had been criticized by some of the philosophers, but their protests had not been widely effective. Some persons vaguely remembered that Xenophanes had accused Homer and Hesiod of attributing to the gods all those actions that are shameful and disgraceful among men, but the intangible monotheism of Xenophanes' way of thinking did not appeal to the popular imagination. The polemic against anthropomorphism was championed by only a few of the later philosophers. Plato had favored the opinion that God does not mingle at all with men but that all intercourse and speech which men have with the deity, whether when they are awake or asleep, is carried on through love. Indeed, love is himself a god who "walks not upon the earth, nor yet upon the skulls of men, which are hard enough, but in the heart and souls of men; in them he walks and dwells and has his home."[6]

The Stoics also, at least in their more strenuous moods, did not take kindly to the notion of specific apparitions of deity. They were content to see the immanent divine presence in all nature about them. As Seneca expressed it, god is the universal intelligence who could be perceived only by thought. He is hidden from our eyes, yet he directs all things in the universe and is in fact himself the greater and better part of his works. One who would appreciate the true greatness of deity will admit that he is all in all, at once within and without his works. And if you ask what is the difference between the divine nature and the human, the proper reply is that in man the better part is spirit, while in god there is nothing except spirit.[7] In later times the Stoic emperor, Marcus Aurelius, conceded that gods might be seen with the human eye, but he insisted that they were to be honored for their works even though they remained unseen. "I have not even seen my own soul," he said, "and yet I honor it. So it is in respect to the gods. From what I constantly experience of their power I know that they exist and I venerate them."[8]

[6] *Symposium* 195; cf. the criticism of Homeric anthropomorphism in the *Republic* 379 ff.

[7] *Natural Questions* i. *Prologue* 13 ff.   [8] *Meditations* xii. 28.

However much philosophers might endeavor to transcendentalize and intellectualize the concept of deity, popular interest moved in the opposite direction. The most effective religions of the day all brought god near to humanity. Often he was said to have been originally a man, like one of the Greek heroes, or a demigod who had once lived heroically on earth. In former times these divinities had been seen by everybody, and, although now they had passed in triumph to the skies, they still manifested themselves in visible form when the occasion might so demand. Yet to look upon the gods was a special privilege not to be indulged in too often or too lightly. One remembered that Homer had once said that it is ill for man to see the gods in bodily shape. There was also the legend about Semele, who had asked Zeus that he show himself to her in the majestic splendor of his Olympian glory, but, when he finally complied with her request, she was consumed by the fiery flames of the lightning that shot forth from this god of thunder. The undimmed effulgence of Zeus was as great a menace to Greeks as was the unveiled brightness of Jehovah's countenance to the Hebrews.

Lesser divinities were more readily visible. Picturesque historical characters, like Alexander the Great, arose to the status of gods and reappeared on earth. After Alexander's death his supernatural personality had been attested by oracular responses, visions, and dreams experienced by various people. On the authority of those who had claimed to have witnessed the phenomenon, the actual *parousia* of the deified Alexander was still an accepted item of current tradition in the second century A.D. According to this story, a spirit exactly resembling the Macedonian prince in form and dress had shown himself in Upper Moesia and Thrace accompanied by a retinue of four hundred attendants equipped with thyrsi and fawnskins. Lodgings and provisions had been furnished the visitants at public expense. Neither governors, soldiers, procurators, nor heads of provinces had dared to offer opposition either by word or by deed. The apparition proceeded "as if in daylight procession prescribed by proclamation," and, after passing to the regions beyond Bithynia, where sacred rites were performed, it finally vanished.[9]

The Romans also had an abundant tradition relative to the visibility of deceased heroic persons. Romulus figured in popular belief as a divinized hero who had later manifested himself on earth. Cicero referred to the subject in a distinctly skeptical vein when he asked for the opinion of his brother Atticus, whose home was near the spot where Romulus was reported to have been seen alive again after his decease. Also Livy seemed somewhat shocked at the readiness with which people accepted this story, but he knew that it had long been the custom to salute Romulus as a god, to implore his favor with prayers, and to honor him with a cult. According to popular belief, Romulus had been snatched away to heaven during a severe thunderstorm. When the disturbance subsided, his throne was found empty. Also a certain Proclus Julius declared to the people that Romulus, suddenly descending from heaven, had appeared at daybreak and said: "Go tell the Romans that the gods so will that my Rome should become the capital of the world. Therefore let them cultivate the art of war and let them know and hand down to posterity that no human power shall be able to withstand the Roman

---

[9] Arrian *Anabasis* vii. 30; Dio Cassius *History* lxxix. 18.

arms. Having said this he ascended up to heaven."[10] Thus an apparition served to give the Roman government its divine commission; on the authority of heaven, Rome was to go into all the world, making subjects of all nations.

Other visitors from heaven were less intimately associated with a previous earthly career, but the reality of their appearance and the help which they rendered were no less highly appreciated. Both Greeks and Romans were fond of claiming the interest of deity in their racial and political welfare. Particularly at critical moments in history had messengers from heaven appeared upon the scene. Poets loved to describe how gods participated in wars and slaughter. The Athenians pictured divinities fighting on their side in the Battle of Marathon. The destruction of the Gauls at Delphi was thought to have been accomplished most manifestly by "the hand of the god and the visible interposition of divinities."[11] Among Romans, too, the same faith prevailed. In Cicero's book on the nature of the gods one of the characters remarked on the belief that Castor and Pollux had been seen fighting in the Roman army on horseback in the war with the Latins. Indeed, he concluded that deities had often appeared in forms so visible that they compelled everybody who was not entirely senseless and hardened in impiety to confess the presence of the gods.

At other times the purpose of an apparition was to demonstrate the favor of heaven for some distinguished human individual. Plutarch sponsors the tradition that the famous Roman dictator Sulla had been visited in a dream by the

---

[10] Cicero Laws i. 1. 3; Livy History i. 16.

[11] Pausanias Itinerary viii. 10. 4; cf. Herodotus History vi. 105 and 117; viii. 38–39 and 65.

Cappadocian goddess Ma, who stood "by him and put into his hand thunder and lightning, then naming his enemies one by one commanded him to strike them." Encouraged by this vision, Sulla marched on victoriously to Rome. Frequently in the case of great men apparitions had served to show that they were a care of the gods, who might wish to insure their divine ancestry or to decree beforehand their reputation for wisdom.

Sometimes quite ordinary mortals were directed in a vision to perform some heaven-assigned task. In one incident an apparition instructed a Roman rustic to inform the Senate that the divinity was displeased with the president of the games. At first the humble peasant feared man more than god and, like the Jonah of Hebrew story, was disobedient to the heavenly vision. When he failed to heed a second warning, he suffered the sudden death of his son. Even after a third vision, he still hesitated and consequently was smitten by a serious illness. Finally, when carried on a litter to the Senate, he discharged his unpleasant but inescapable task and at once completely recovered his health.

Demonic powers also claimed a place for themselves in the world of visions. Even though the demon was merely the spirit of a dead man, when it entered the sphere of the supernatural, it assumed the prerogatives of a divinity. In one such instance an actual cult had shaped itself around a much-dreaded figure that was popularly reputed to be the ghost of one of the sailors of Odysseus. When the Trojan warrior came to the small town of Temesa in southern Italy, the natives killed one of his drunken sailors for violence done to a maiden of the town. The ghost of the dead man then took revenge upon the natives by killing many of their number.

Not until they were advised by the Pythian priestess to build a temple to the ghost and to make provision for his satisfaction did he cease his depredations. But finally the boxer Euthymus, appearing upon the scene, girded himself for a conflict with the specter, who was so real that a mortal could actually engage him in a physical combat. As a result, the demon was driven into the sea, never to return, but his form was well remembered. Pausanias, who tells the story, had seen a portrait said to be a copy of an old painting in which the ghost was represented as of a horrid black color with a most dreadful appearance.[12] From writing on the picture his name was known to be Lycas. The vision of Lycas descending headlong into the sea was as real for the gentile reader of the Gospel of Luke as were the evangelist's stories about Satan falling as lightning from heaven or about demonized swine plunging to death in the Lake of Gennesaret.

Notorious characters, like the infamous Nero, also readily played the role of divinities in apparitional imagery. When the author of Revelation spoke of the beast who once was, but no longer is, and is about to come up out of the abyss, his contemporaries would have no difficulty in recalling the popular legend that had already connected itself with this most vicious of emperors. Even during his lifetime, if Plutarch—who was a contemporary of John of Patmos—is correctly informed, Nero's enormities had led the Roman people to suspect that he was "no human creature but some penal or vindictive supernatural power that had seized the Empire."[13] After his death there quickly arose the belief that he would return to

---

[12] *Itinerary* vi. 6. 3–4.

[13] Plutarch *Otho*. ii.

take vengeance on his enemies. When Suetonius was a young man, an impostor who claimed to be Nero had appeared among the Parthians, and many people were quite ready to accept his pretensions.[14]

Christians could unhesitatingly accept the Neronic tradition, since they could set over against the heathen's faith the bolder and more triumphant hope of a reappearance of their own hero, the Lord Jesus Christ. He would conquer and hurl down to eternal perdition the imperial monster with all his demonic attendants. This ultimate apparition of Christ would thus demonstrate the final victory and full truth of the new religion. In general, Christians found it exceedingly advantageous to adopt and revise the apparitional imagery so widely current in their gentile environment.

[14] Suetonius *Nero* lvii.

CHAPTER III
CHANNELS OF REVELATION

THE supernatural world impinged upon the life of people within the Roman Empire in a great variety of ways. Not everybody's eye was sufficiently sensitive to register visions of the gods, angels, demons, or ghosts that were commonly believed to frequent the haunts of mortals. Although the reality of apparitions might be accepted without question, communications with the supernal regions were by no means limited to this single area of experience. Even among Christians there were many persons who had never been privileged to see an angel, much less to witness a vision of the risen Jesus. Nor did apparitions, numerous as they were, furnish mankind with an adequately full disclosure of divine wisdom and inspiration for every contingency in life. It was necessary to tap other and more readily accessible sources of help. These were not wanting. At the time of Christianity's rise the inhabitants of the Roman world were accustomed to seek and find divine guidance in many different quarters. The channels of revelation were varied and abundant.

I

Many people were expert in reading the signs of the times. For Gentiles, as well as for Jews and Christians, the heavens declared the glory of god, and one saw in the revealing features of nature's face knowledge of the divine forces behind all phenomena. Cicero put into the mouth of the Stoic Lucilius words that were acceptable to large numbers of persons in that day: "What can be so plain and evident, when we behold the heavens and contemplate the celestial bodies, as the existence of some pre-eminently intelligent divinity by whom all things are governed."[1]

There were said to be four principal kinds of divine revelation that stand written for every man on the face of nature. In the first place, there is that foreknowledge of future events which the gods have intrusted to certain individuals. The augur, if a genuine performer, is a chosen instrument of deity to show men the signs of future happenings. The second type of revelation is the manifest kindness of providence displayed in nature. In the salubrious climate of the Mediterranean area, in the fertility of the earth and the variety of its products, the intelligent man would recognize the expression of the divine favor for humanity. The terrible side of nature was also useful to man in his efforts to read the will of the gods. Thunder, tempests, earthquakes, showers of stones and rain like drops of blood, monstrous births of men and beasts, and meteors shooting across the heavens were all divine forebodings of impending calamities. In the fourth place, the stable and orderly side of nature was no less significant for divine revelation. No intelligent person, it was thought, could regard as the result of mere chance the regularity with which the heavenly bodies followed their courses, the beauty of the sun and the moon, and the glory of the starry night. Such perfection could have come into being only through the opera-

[1] *Nature of the Gods* ii. 2.

tion of a supremely divine intelligence. Here was an open book of revelation ready for every man to read.

The philosopher might be able to find a satisfactory revelation of the deity by reflecting upon the beneficence of a kindly providence and the magnificence of an orderly cosmos, but the average man felt ill at ease in so rarefied an atmosphere. When he wanted to know the meaning of nature—and he always desired this knowledge—he consulted a professional augur in the hope of discovering hidden meanings in portentous happenings. It was a generally accepted belief that the gods, since they knew in advance everything that would take place, could forecast the consequences of any decision that an individual might make. Also, the divinities were assumed to be friendly and ready when duly consulted to intimate by omens, dreams, auguries, or other revelatory signs the line of conduct that one should pursue or avoid. It was said that he who chose to obey the revealed will of the deities would never have occasion to regret his decision, but disobedience would be attended by inevitable punishment.

Numerous forms of divination were popular among both Greeks and Romans. The divine mind was found revealed in the flight of birds, in the action of lightning, in the entrails of a sacrificed victim, and in many other signs known to the professional diviner. The casting of lots was a custom widely practiced even by Christians. When they desired divine guidance in selecting a successor to Judas, they asked God to indicate his choice by use of the lots. This was a procedure that the gentile reader of Acts would readily understand.

It was a widely established belief among both Jews and Gentiles that no momentous occurrence ever had or ever would come to pass without appropriate warnings from the deity. Jewish opinion on this subject was given most striking expression in the description of premonitory signs to precede the end of the world. The stars would deviate from their course, the moon would shine in the daytime, and the sun would suddenly burst out in the night. Fire would fall from heaven or break forth from the ground, and terrible earthquakes would occur. The seasons would be altered and the year shortened. Rain would cease, and drought and famine would result. Terrible apparitions would be seen in the heavens—open books which all might read, flaming swords, and battling giants. On earth, rocks and trees would drip blood, stones would cry out, and all nature would be out of joint. These and vast numbers of similar phenomena would reveal to man the approach of the final catastrophe.

Even less terrible events were preceded by appropriate portents. Josephus lists the prodigies that had foreshadowed the fall of Jerusalem in A.D. 70. A star resembling a sword had stood over the city, and for a whole year a comet had been visible. At the Passover feast immediately preceding the war, at three o'clock in the morning for half an hour so great a light shone around the altar and the holy house that it appeared to be bright daytime. At the same festival a heifer, as she was being led by the high priest to be sacrificed, brought forth a lamb in the court of the temple. The eastern gate of the inner court, though so heavy that it required twenty men to close it, opened of its own accord about midnight. A few days after the feast, before sunset, chariots and troops of soldiers in their armor were seen running about among the clouds. Reflecting upon these signs, Josephus remarks: "Now if any one consider these things he will find that God takes care of mankind and by all ways possible foreshadows to our race what is for their preservation."[2]

Likewise among the Greeks and Romans portents were highly rated as indications of heaven's will in connection with momentous events. Livy recounts a formidable array of prodigies preceding the defeat of the Romans by Hannibal. It was reported from Sicily that several darts belonging to the soldiers had taken fire, and in Sardinia the staff of a horseman who was going on his rounds upon the wall burst into flame as he held it in his hand. The shores had blazed with frequent fires. Two shields had sweated blood. At Praeneste red-hot stones had fallen from the heavens, and at Arpi shields were seen in the sky and the sun fought with the moon. At Capena two moons rose in the daytime, and the waters of Caere had flowed mixed with blood. The statue of Mars at Rome had sweated at the sight of images of wolves. At Capua the heavens were seen on fire and the moon appeared to be falling amidst rain. Still other prodigies of less magnitude had also been observed.[3]

A series of similar warnings had, it was said, been experienced by Julius Caesar prior to his assassination. Shortly before his death he had been told that the horses which, upon his crossing the Rubicon, he had consecrated and turned loose to graze without a keeper abstained entirely from eating and shed floods of tears. The soothsayer Spurinna also noted ominous appearances in the sacrifices. Caesar had dreamed that he was soaring above the clouds, and his wife had

[2] *War* vi. 5. 3–4.
[3] Livy *History* xxii. 1.

dreamed that her husband had been stabbed and had fallen upon her bosom. Such were the ways in which the gods had endeavored to convey warnings to Caesar, and after his death their displeasure was made plain by further portentous happenings. The sun, being unwilling to view the horrid crime, turned away its light and continued to shine with dimmed splendor. It failed to show its ordinary radiance at its rising, and its heat was diminished during the whole year. On the other hand, the divine favor toward Caesar was shown by the elevation of his soul to the heavens, where it shone brightly in the form of a new comet for seven nights in succession.[4]

In a similar vein Dio Cassius referred to signs preceding Domitian's assassination, remarking that no occurrence of such magnitude is without previous indications. Domitian in a dream beheld the assassin approaching him with a sword. He also dreamed that Minerva, whose statue he kept in his bedchamber, threw away her weapons, mounted a chariot drawn by black horses, and disappeared in an abyss. But, most wonderful of all, a prophet named Proclus had foretold in Germany the very day on which the event was to occur. Even when brought into the presence of the emperor and faced with the threat of death, he still reiterated the prophecy, and the event happened as predicted in spite of the emperor's precautions.[5]

Christians also made much of portents as an indication of the divine will. They repeated Jewish imagery regarding events to precede the end of the world, and they borrowed the

[4] Suetonius *Julius Caesar* lxxxi; cf. Vergil *Georgics* i. 466 ff.; Josephus *Antiquities* xiv. 12. 3; Plutarch *Caesar* lxiii ff.; Strabo *Fragment* 14 (Müller, III, 494).

[5] Dio Cassius *History* lxvii. 16.

vivid language of Old Testament apocalyptic prophecy. There would be great tribulation, with wars and rumors of wars, earthquakes in many places, and deadly famines. Blood and fire and vapor of smoke would cover the heavens and the earth, and the sun would be turned into darkness, as the day approached for the triumphant return of Jesus to enact the final judgment and set up his kingdom on the renovated earth.

Predictions of events yet to be revealed were supplemented by citation of portents from the past. This procedure was especially congenial to Gentiles, and the Christian preacher in gentile lands was ready to cater to this interest. The star of Bethlehem, which had guided the Magi, bespoke the interest of heaven in the appearance of Jesus on earth. The will of God regarding his unique personality had been uttered verbally from the upper regions at his baptism and again on the mount of transfiguration. His entire career had been a display of mighty works and wonders and signs which God did by him in the presence of men. And, finally, at his death the sun hid its face, the earth quaked, the veil of the temple was torn in two, the rocks were rent, the tombs were opened, and many bodies of dead saints came forth. Thus Christianity proved to be not at all inferior to Jewish or to gentile faith in the use of portents as a medium by which the will of the deity had been communicated to mankind.

II

The sacred book was an important source of supernatural wisdom for many persons in the ancient world. Among Jews inspired scripture had early attained a position of unique respect. It was taken to be a verbally accurate record from which the revealed will of God in all things could be learned. The Gentiles also had their own mysterious books that were sources of supernatural power when used by a competent person. By the beginning of the Christian Era there were in circulation, particularly in the eastern Mediterranean lands, large numbers of writings containing formulas whose divine potency was supposed to be efficacious over a wide range of human experience. These books contained recipes for casting out demons, for healing all sorts of diseases, for insuring safety in various undertakings, and for rendering assistance in every imaginable emergency.

The practice of magic, except by properly authorized persons, was severely censured and sometimes strictly forbidden. In an ideal society Plato would impose the death penalty on a public prophet or diviner who resorted to its use, and a private magician would be liable to punishment according to the measure of the injury which had resulted from the practice of his art. But the supernatural efficacy of magic seems to have been universally conceded. It was thought possible to obtain formulas of adjuration or petition that, when correctly repeated, would force even the gods to do one's bidding. Many persons must have been severely tempted to seek the acquisition of the books that were supposed to yield this superhuman wisdom.

Among the Romans it was the business of the pontiff to keep himself fully informed on what formula was to be used for any required occasion. Not only was success in war assured but farming and health were safeguarded by the recital of magical phrases. One treated a sore on the body by placing the

hand in a prescribed manner upon the afflicted spot and recit-
ing: "Depart, whether produced today or aforetime, whether
created today or aforetime; this plague, this pestilence, this
pain, this tumor, this inflammation, these goiters, these tonsils,
this bunch, these swellings, this scrofula, this blotch, I call
forth, I draw out, I exorcise by means of this magic from these
limbs and marrow."[6] In private hands an instrument of this
sort was easily misused, and it was not a simple matter for the
law to control one who possessed this magical skill. It is not
surprising that books containing a great variety of formulas
should have been much in demand and widely circulated.
When the Christian missionaries succeeded in persuading the
heathen to trust simply in the all-efficacious name of Jesus for
divine protection from human ills, it would have been easily
possible to find in the new converts' possession magical books
for a bonfire like that staged one day in Ephesus (Acts 19:18–
19).

The numerous magical papyri that have been exhumed
from the rubbish heaps of the Roman East give point to the
statement of Pliny the Elder that, of all the arts known in his
day, magic was the most influential and had exerted its baneful influence over the legitimate arts of divination, medicine,
and religion. In the opinion of Pliny the pernicious practice
had come from Persia, where its literature had originated with
some "two millions of verses" from the hand of Zoroaster.
Democritus was charged with having encouraged the art
among the Greeks by alleging that the tomb of Dardanus
contained writings for this purpose and in agreement with
which Democritus produced a further literature about the

[6] Marcellus *Remedies* xv. 11.

time of the Peloponnesian War. Pliny accuses Jews also of contributing to the perverted custom, the persons most responsible having been "Moses, Jannes and Lotapea." Evidently the high estimate placed upon a sacred book among the Jews, as well as among the Persians, lent color to the charge that these peoples were natural adepts in the magic art.[7]

The Jewish philosopher Philo tried to divert suspicion from his fellow-Jews by affirming that holy inspiration could not live in the same house with magic. Nevertheless, evidence is not lacking to indicate that there were expert Jewish magicians. The Essenes had, in addition to the regular Hebrew Scriptures, other secret holy books by the use of which they were reputed to be exceptionally successful in divination.[8] And individual Jews, like Simon in Samaria and Elymas at Paphos,[9] already enjoyed a reputation as successful magicians before Christian missionaries proclaimed among Gentiles the superior efficacy of the name of Jesus.

Among the Romans the use of sacred formulas under the official direction of the state was a highly prized procedure. The Roman people had long been in possession of holy books that were believed to constitute an infallible source of information for ascertaining the will of the gods. The origin of heathen Rome's canon of scriptures is veiled in obscurity, but, where facts were lacking, fancy filled the gap. Legend reported that an old woman came to King Tarquin with a collection of nine books of Sibylline oracles, presumably from Cumae, which she offered to sell for a stated price. At first the

---

[7] Pliny *Natural History* xxx. 1 ff.

[8] Josephus *War* ii. 8. 7 and 12.

[9] Acts 8:9 ff.; 13:6 ff.

king refused to purchase the books. But after she had burned six of them in his presence, he relented and purchased the remaining three at the original price asked for the nine. At first they were intrusted to two guardians, but later the number was raised to ten and finally to fifteen, who held office for life. No one else had access to this sacred collection, which was kept in the crypt of the Capitoline Temple and might be consulted only by the "Fifteen Men."

When the Capitol was burned in 83 B.C., the precious documents perished, but fortunately Cumae was not the only home of an oracular priestess. In ancient times the Greeks appear to have known only one Sibyl, but by the fourth century B.C. there were at least three, and the Roman Varro in the first century B.C. spoke categorically of ten. Consequently, after the destruction of the original Roman collection, the Senate decreed that a new collection should be made from all available sources and the whole submitted to the priests, who were to sift the genuine from the spurious. Thus a new official document was procured and endowed with all the sanctity of the old.

From time to time the authorities adopted measures for suppressing any oracular books thought unorthodox or likely to rival the official collection. But after the fire of 83 B.C. additions to the accepted canon were admitted more freely when these were properly attested. The new oracles had to show Sibylline credentials, otherwise they were consigned to the flames. This was the motive that prompted Augustus in the course of his reforms to destroy the two thousand volumes mentioned by Suetonius. Whether these rival books were in Latin or in Greek, if their authors were unknown or of no great authority, the documents were burned. Only those officially approved were spared. They were inclosed in a gilded box and deposited under the pedestal of the statue of Palatine Apollo.[10]

Under Tiberius, the successor of Augustus, the same care was exercised in admitting books into the Sibylline canon. On one occasion a member of the College of Fifteen petitioned the Senate to allow a certain writing to be included in the official collection. A young tribune made a motion to that effect, and the matter was passed without comment. But, when Tiberius heard of the proceedings, he criticized the parties concerned for putting through so important a motion without giving it due publicity. He excused the tribune who made the motion on the ground of his youth and lack of familiarity with ancient usage, but he upbraided the member of the pontifical college who had first suggested the move. The emperor's objection was based upon the fact that the author of the document in question was not known, that the consent of the entire college had not been obtained, and that the motion had not been given the proper reading and deliberation in the Senate but had been passed in a thin house.[11]

From the outset Christians had entertained the idea of revelation in a sacred book, which they took over from Judaism. The Bible of the earliest Christians was identical with that of their Jewish kinsmen, although it was interpreted to suit the special needs of the new religion. Christians also wrote letters to friends and to churches for the purpose of furthering the new cause, and they assembled traditions about the life of

[10] Suetonius *Augustus* xxxi.
[11] Tacitus *Annals* vi. 12.

Jesus for the edification of different persons and communities. But at first there was no disposition to include these distinctively Christian documents in the category of sacred Scripture. It was not until the second century A.D. that they were assembled into a canon and given a place beside the original collection of Jewish books. And then it was the Romans, with their inherited genius for sifting the spurious from the genuine, and thus safeguarding orthodoxy, who led in the movement. Ultimately it was not so much the Jewish Palestinian conception of a body of ancient religious books as the old Roman idea of a Sibylline canon that came to prevail in the Christian church. The application of the test of orthodoxy, the insistence upon a particular class of authorship such as that of apostles or near-apostles, the suppression of documents that did not conform to official standards, and the withholding of the Scriptures from the laity were all a distinctively Roman rather than a Jewish inheritance within the early church.

III

Another notable source of revelation was the inspired person, an idea essentially more primitive than that of the inspired book. There were two main classes of such persons: (1) those who were taught of God and (2) those who were filled with God.

One of the oldest forms in which the divinely instructed man appears is that of lawgiver. Among the Hebrews, Moses had been chosen to receive the law from God, even as in earlier times the Babylonian Hammurabi received his famous code from the sun-god. But the peoples of the Greco-Roman world were not dependent on the Semites for the figure of the divinely instructed lawgiver. It was also true of the Greeks that they respected divine in preference to human law. Minos of Crete and Lycurgus of Sparta were said to have consulted Zeus at regular intervals to ascertain the type of legislation to be enacted under their respective jurisdictions. Among the Romans the Twelve Tables were a strictly human creation, but they embodied materials from earlier codes that had been promulgated by leaders who administered justice as impartially "as if from an oracle." Moreover, the actual genesis of Roman law was believed to have been much older, its real founder having been Numa, who was wise as any man could be in all laws "both divine and human," and ruled the people by "religious devices and divine law."[12]

In Christian teaching Jesus was the new lawgiver uttering the genuine oracles of God. He was presented to Jews as a second Moses who supplemented the older revelation; they of olden times had taught so-and-so, but now the final word had been spoken by Jesus. But, when Christianity spread to gentile lands, the figure of the divine teacher, communicating to men the wisdom that he had learned from the deity, would not have seemed at all strange. In fact, the form in which the collections of Jesus' teaching were best known in the early days is not that of "laws" (*nomoi*) or "teaching" (*didache*) but "oracles" (*logia*), the term used of the oracular responses received by the heathen lawgivers and passed on by them to mankind.

Closely related to the lawgiver stood the prophet. He had two chief though kindred functions: he conveyed instruction from God to men and he foretold events. That is, he exhorted

---

[12] Livy *History* i. 18; iii. 34; Tacitus *Annals* iii. 26.

and he predicted. He differed from the lawgiver in that the latter mediated a set body of revelation, whereas the prophet's revelation was more fluid. He brought revelation down to date, so to speak.

The prophet figured very prominently in all the religions of the Greco-Roman world. With his importance for the Hebrews everyone is familiar, but among the Greeks, the Romans, and the Christians he occupied a similarly significant place. Strabo remarks that Hindus, Persians, Assyrians, Greeks, and Romans thought prophets even worthy of thrones, because both during their lifetime and after their death they were supposed to communicate ordinances and precepts from the gods. They spoke with the authority of deity behind their words, whether it was the Hebrew Isaiah exclaiming, "Thus said Jehovah," or the Roman Marcius proclaiming, "Thus spake Jupiter."[13] Frequently, as with the Hebrews, the activity of the prophet was connected with the political warfare of the people. Thus the famous Greek leader Epaminondas had been incited by the prophecies of Bacis to lead the Messenians in their efforts to recover their lost territory. Both Bacis and a predecessor named Euclus had prophesied with reference to the conflict between the Greeks and the Persians. As late as the second century A.D. the works of several of these prophets were still extant. Several of them are listed by Pausanias, who had read most of their oracles. The Greeks also recognized prophetic women, like Deborah of early Hebrew tradition. To the many well-known Sibylline prophetesses one may add Phaennis, daughter of the king of the

[13] Strabo *Geography* xvi. 2. 39; Livy *History* xxv. 12.

Chaonians, and the Peleae of Dodona, whose fame was known to Pausanias.[14]

The role of the prophet among the early Christians was an important one. When instructing the Corinthians regarding the order of preferment among the officials of the new community, Paul remarked that "God hath set some in the church first apostles, secondly prophets, thirdly teachers" (I Cor. 12:28). Next to the apostles, whose number was limited, stood the prophet as the foremost individual in the Christian community. Also the ability to prophesy was the one spiritual gift toward the attainment of which every Christian should strive. Yet Paul would not tolerate prophetesses, for he gave orders that women should keep silence in the churches. He did not propose to have a Christian Sibyl. But other Christian communities apparently were more tolerant. We learn from Acts 21:8-9 that Philip the evangelist who resided at Caesarea had four daughters, all of them prophetesses.

The figure of the Christian prophet mediating the divine revelation, sometimes in hortatory address and sometimes in specific predictions, was in many respects a more natural phenomenon among Gentiles than among Jews. Although Christians drew heavily upon the old Hebrew prophets for proof-texts in their preaching, the Christian prophets did not aim to reproduce the ancient type. Their activities pertained to the immediate situation and answered the demand of their contemporary environment. In the Greco-Roman world the professional exhorter in the form of the Cynic-Stoic preacher, and the professional forecaster of events (the diviner), were to be met on almost every street corner, both claiming to have

[14] *Itinerary* iv. 27. 4; x. 12. 5; 14. 6.

a divine message to deliver to mankind. Christians entered
the lists with these competitors and ultimately won from them
on their own ground.

The prophet was not merely taught of God, but in many
instances he was inhabited by some sort of divine increment in
his being. This idea was particularly conspicuous among the
early Hebrews. When God took a part of the Spirit with
which he had endowed Moses and put it on the seventy elders,
they also prophesied. Saul had become a prophet when the
Spirit of God came mightily upon him. When Elijah died, he
passed on this divine gift to Elisha, but Elisha was less successful in transmitting it to King Joash. The prophet, because of
his divine equipment, was especially the "man of God." He
was "the man that hath the Spirit" which so overmastered
him that people said the prophet is a "fool," he is "mad."
Similarly the great literary prophets uttered their message
when the Spirit of the Lord came upon them. Filled with
God, so to speak, they gave vent to the divine urge in their
words of revelation spoken and recorded for the guidance of
their hearers or readers.

The same type of divine impulsion characterized the prophets and prophetesses among the Greeks and Romans. The
devotees of Dionysus experienced, in the ecstasy accompany-
ing the Bacchic frenzy, the prophetic gift of this deity, "for in
all fulness when he floods our frame he makes his maddened
votaries tell the future." Speaking of the Cumaean Sibyl,
Vergil says: "The prophetess raves with wild outrage in the
cave struggling if possible to unburden her soul of the mighty
god." She was actually frenzied with prophetic inspiration.
Similarly the Sibyl at Delphi uttered her oracles under the

frenzy and inspiration of the god. Also Euclus the Cyprian, Musaeus the Athenian, Lycus son of Pandion, and Bacis the Boeotian are said to have "prophesied by the inspiration of god."[15]

Even the philosophers recognized the divinity of prophetic frenzy and called it a "madness which is the special gift of heaven and the source of chiefest blessings among men." Rationality was a merely human characteristic, while prophetic madness was of divine origin. Thus it happened that the prophetesses at Delphi and at Dodona in their normal moments had been of no significance, but, when frenzied by divine inspiration, they had been the source of inestimable good for both the public and the private affairs of the Greeks.

Among the Romans prophetic inspiration was taken for granted.[16] Yet there were some critics who doubted whether the verses of the Sibyl had really been uttered under the impulsion of frenzy. The acrostic arrangement and other artifices evident in these poems seemed to indicate that they had been the work of a more sober technical skill. But the Gentiles in the first and second Christian centuries still generally believed, even though the oracles were then falling into decay, that prophetic frenzy was a genuinely divine gift to humanity. The revered Heraclitus was still cited in support of the Sibyl "who with frenzied mouth utters words unmirthful, unadorned, untricked, and reaches with her voice through a thousand years by the agency of god."[17]

When Christians preached the doctrine of their prophets'

---

[15] On this phenomenon see Euripides *Bacchanals* 298 ff.; Vergil *Aeneid* vi. 42 ff.; Pausanias *Itinerary* i. 12. 1; x. 12. 5; cf. Plato *Phaedrus* 244.

[16] See Vergil *Aeneid* vi. 77 ff.; Pliny *Natural History* vii. 33; Lucan *Pharsalia* v. 165 ff.; Tacitus *Annals* ii. 54.

[17] Plutarch *Pythian Oracles* vi; cf. *Cessation of Oracles* xi.

divine infilling, they were fitting their thought into a familiar gentile pattern. The Corinthians would take readily to Paul's explanation of prophecy as due to endowment by a divine spirit. Also in Acts 19:6 one reads that after certain converts were baptized, and Paul had laid his hands on them, they received the Holy Spirit and prophesied in consequence of this new equipment. When predicting the imprisonment awaiting Paul on his visit to Jerusalem, Agabus sealed his own words with the remark: "Thus saith the Holy Spirit." The Christian prophet was a possessed person; he was inhabited by a divine potency called the Holy Spirit.

Great poets and philosophers were often regarded as inspired persons who thus served as channels of revelation for their contemporaries and descendants. God, it was said, so takes away the minds of poets that beautiful poems are the utterances of the divine wisdom, the very words of the deity, spoken for the edification of mankind. Plato had said that the writer who imagines that he can by art, and without any "touch of madness in his soul," enter the sanctuary of the Muse, will find himself rejected. Poetic language owed its beauty to the divine afflatus with which the poet was endowed. The author was like a servant in the sacred mysteries who stood without, ministering at the altar, and to whom there came from within the sanctuary an inspiration, a flash of truth, like a sudden beam of light shooting out from an invisible fire. In the case of Homer, his inspiration had been so great that it was thought as impossible to improve upon one of his lines as it was to detract from the fire of Zeus or the club of Hercules.[18]

[18] For these ideas one may consult Plato *Phaedrus* 245; *Theaetetus* 194; *Ion* 530 ff.; Democritus *Fragment* 18 (Diels); Dio Chrysostom *Oration* xxxvi. 33–34; Macrobius *Saturnalia* v. 3.

Likewise the great philosopher was a man who had forgotten earthly interests and had become rapt in the divine. The vulgar person might rebuke him for insanity, but that was because the common man was incapable of appreciating the philosopher's inspiration. It was a superhuman insert in man that made possible the accomplishment of all noble thinking and all eloquence of speech. No man was ever great without a measure of the "divine afflatus."[19]

The Greek doctrine of inspiration survived and continued to be reaffirmed well into early Christian times. In the first quarter of the second century A.D. the doctrine was given emphatic expression by Dio Chrysostom. He rated all wisdom emanating from the natural man as relatively worthless in comparison with the utterances of those inspired and prophetic figures through whom the gods had spoken. All wisdom and truth possessed by mankind regarding the gods and the universe had come, in the opinion of Dio, not from human reason but from a revelation of the divine will and from decrees made known through the medium of prophetic and divine men of old.

Not everybody demanded that all inspired men should have belonged among the ancients. Rather, the experience repeated itself continuously in the life of anyone who showed an aptitude for responding to the will of the gods. One could never know when the afflatus would be available, but, when it struck, it meant a fresh insert of the divine into the area of the human. For the Jews the most significant displays of revela-

[19] Plato *Phaedrus* 249; *Timaeus* 72; Cicero *Tusculan* i. 26; *Nature of the Gods* ii. 66.

tion had been in the past, but Gentiles were less rigidly bound to the authority of antiquity. Philo of Alexandria was more Gentile than Jew in this area of his thinking. He contrasted the relative futility of normal mental effort with those occasions when inspiration, taking violent hold on one, temporarily dethroned the puny human mind. He marveled at the manner in which God on occasion filled the soul with wisdom. Philo did not blush to narrate that such experiences had happened to him "ten thousand times."[20]

For Christians also inspiration was both ancient and immediate. Very early in the history of the new religion it became a uniformly accepted belief that God had spoken quite as authoritatively in the message of Jesus as in the ancient Scriptures. Even in the promptings of their own pious convictions Christians found a message of revelation for men of their contemporary world. When lacking a passage of Scripture or a command of Jesus to cite in support of an opinion, Paul could speak on his own authority as one who possessed the mind of Christ, even the Spirit of God. When the missionary met forceful opposition, he relied not on his own feeble words spoken in self-defense but upon the language that would be supplied by the Holy Spirit in the hour of crisis. In the displays of ecstasy within their communities Christians felt themselves to be channels of divine power by which God was communicating his will anew to mankind. Undoubtedly this conviction had been greatly stimulated by similar notions of the immediacy of revelation current in the gentile environment of Christianity. In this respect its rivals had to be surpassed.

[20] *Care of Divine Things* liii; *Migration of Abraham* vii.

IV

(Another source of divine help highly prized by the Greeks
was the activity of beings intermediate between gods and
men. This class of inferior divinity was best known by the
term "demon" (*daimon*). The Christian notion that all
demons were evil was Jewish rather than Greek imagery. In
Greek thinking the demons were primarily kindly, serving
the interests of a needy humanity.] Their power was higher
than that of man but lower than that of the mighty gods.
Hesiod, giving literary dress to popular mythology, depicted
the demons as benevolent powers who haunted the earth,
traveling hither and yon and wrapping themselves in mist in
order that, unperceived, they might render assistance to mankind. They were said to be the souls of men who had lived
in the Golden Age and who by their native superior powers
were particularly well suited to their intermediate role. Thrice
ten thousand in number, they served as the watchers of Zeus
over mortal men.[21] Socrates, taking over the imagery of
Hesiod, affirmed that the souls of deceased men of the Golden
Age had become "holy demons on earth, beneficent averters
of ills, guardians of mortals." The guardian demon was a
daily companion and guide who so communicated his wisdom and goodness to the object of his care that every virtuous
man might properly be called a "demonized" person. The
philosopher did not deny the existence of both good and bad
demons, but he preferred to dwell more extensively on the
benevolent aspects of the intermediaries' functions.[22]

[21] Hesiod *Works and Days* 122 ff., 251 ff.; see also the "Hymn to Musaeus,"
11. 30 ff., in Thomas Taylor, *Mystical Hymns of Orpheus*, p. 5.

[22] Plato *Cratylus* 397–98; Plutarch *Cessation of Oracles* xvii; *Isis and Osiris* xlv ff.

The guardian spirit that had watched over Socrates was a favorite theme on many occasions. The demon was said to have led Socrates in all the actions of his life, presiding over and by divine instinct directing his thoughts. The popular notion that the demon actually dwelt within man seemed untenable to the Platonic philosopher, but he allowed it to be a kind of divine double that stood above one, ministering to one's needs. Or perhaps it was a kind of superior soul with which the deity had endowed man. It resided in the head as the rational principle constantly pulling the soul godward. In this role the demon served, much as did the Holy Spirit, or Wisdom, or Logos among Jews and Christians with Platonic leanings, to span the gulf that must of necessity separate the realms of the gods from the abodes of men.

The manner in which revelation was mediated by demonic powers might vary. From the point of view of a strict Platonist or an older Stoic, one could not permit them any very great freedom to display extraordinary and independent supernatural activities. Other interpreters made these intermediary beings responsible for the revelations and miracles of the magician, or they inspired the diviner and the prophet. Probably Apuleius advocated a widely popular view of the second century A.D. when he called demons the messengers between the inhabitants of earth and those of heaven. Although everything happens by the will and power of the celestial gods, the intermediate agency in accomplishing their will is one or another of the many demons who are busy journeying back and forth over the space separating the immortals from mankind. In fact, such knowledge as is communicated through the verses of the sibyls, through predictions of the augurs, and through all sorts of portents and dreams, is thought by Apulcius to find its only legitimate explanation in the theory of intermediary agencies.[23]

When demons failed to act of their own accord, devices were available for compelling their services. The magician with his spells, charms, and powerful formulas came to the rescue. In this connection he was chiefly significant on account of his assumed ability to obtain revelations from the dead by skill in necromancy. He would, for a fee, bring up from Hades one's recently deceased relative, or an ancient person of renown, from whom he pretended to obtain information about matters lying beyond the range of normal human knowledge. Plato would have jailed all magicians who claimed ability to conjure the dead; he said they would utterly demolish whole houses and states for the sake of money. But necromancers continued for many centuries to be in demand even in aristocratic circles. The practice of the art by a certain Junius had been the undoing of a pretor in the time of Tiberius. Nero had sought the aid of men of this craft in bringing up his mother's ghost in order to allay her anger against him, and Caracalla had vainly endeavored to obtain a message from enchanted spirits to cure the diseases and distressing dreams from which he suffered.[24]

The gentile reader whom the author of Luke addressed would have felt no difficulty in assuming that the deceased Lazarus could have returned to earth to warn the rich brothers of Dives, although Theophilus might have wondered why the

[23] *God of Socrates* vi.

[24] See Plato *Laws* 909; Pliny *Natural History* xxx. 2 (6); Lucan *Pharsalia* vi. 430 ff.; Tacitus *Annals* ii. 28; Suetonius *Nero* xxxiv. 4; Dio Cassius *History* lxxvii. 15.

request was not made to a professional necromancer instead of to Abraham. But neither Jews nor Christians encouraged interest in this form of commerce with supernatural powers. Intermediary agents of the upper world were too abundant and too easy of access to make necessary any extensive practice of the necromantic art.

Philo of Alexandria endeavored to equate Jewish and gentile belief in the activity of intermediaries by means of his doctrine of angels. According to Philo, those beings whom the Greeks called demons had been called angels by Moses. They were invisible souls that hovered about in the air. Some of them were kindly disposed toward men, while others were malevolent. As the Gentile spoke of good and evil demons, meaning good and evil souls ever present but imperceptible to normal vision, so the Jew spoke of good and evil angels. To recognize that souls, demons, and angels were in reality identical would, Philo thought, relieve the heathen of the great burden of superstition from which they were suffering. It was God himself who had filled the world with intermediary incorporeal beings; hence their beneficent activities were simply a phase of his operations. In minds that had been thoroughly purified by reason God himself presided, but in the minds of those persons who had not yet attained to so high a degree of perfection angels continued to serve as God's representative. Thus Philo sought to preserve the ideal of Jewish monotheism, while recognizing current gentile belief in intermediaries.[25]

Christians were less troubled about harmonizing Jewish and gentile modes of thinking. They conceded without ques-

[25] *Giants* ii–iv; *Dreams* i. 22–23.

tion the existence of demons, together with both good and bad angels. There were intermediary agents sponsored by God as well as by Satan, and the activities of both groups had been extensively displayed in connection with the career of Jesus and the experiences of his followers during the early years of the new religion's history. Angelic mediators of good were especially frequent as helpers and instructors in supernatural wisdom, and thus Christianity in the course of time equipped itself to meet a widely current demand of the Gentiles. Moreover, angels were secondary to the new intermediary power recognized in the person of the risen Jesus, who continually led and protected his followers. As Holy Spirit, Comforter, divine Logos, he exercised a never failing care over the faithful. He stood between them and God, serving as their advocate in heaven and their guardian on earth. In this role he was capable of supplanting and transcending all rival intermediaries in whom the heathen had been accustomed to trust.

CHAPTER IV
THE FUNCTION OF HEROIC SAVIORS

THE presence of friendly supernatural forces working on behalf of mankind was most vividly and effectively depicted by the figure of the ancient hero. He was the ideal mediator between gods and men. By means of his activities the hard lot of mortals was relieved and evil destiny averted. He redeemed them from all sorts of limitations, dangers, and misfortunes. He knew the needs of men because he himself had formerly shared human experiences on earth, even to the extent of partcipating in the agonies of death. But his triumph had been complete even over the grave. After his departure from earth, he passed to heaven, where he acquired the status and character of a genuine divinity. His popularity was in evidence all about the Mediterranean long before Christianity arose. Probably no religious impulse among the peoples of the Roman Empire in the first century of the Christian Era was stronger than the disposition to seek supernatural aid through the mediation of one or another type of heroic savior.

I

The gentile contemporaries of the early Christians were abundantly supplied with a great variety of divine helpers who while on earth had rendered exceptional aid to mankind and after death continued to serve still more effectively all who trusted in them. During their earthly career they had been highly endowed persons who, as patrons of civilization, founders of cities, teachers of agriculture, leaders of armies, skilful physicians, powerful athletes, brilliant poets, or profound philosophers, had proved so superior to the average run of men that they had from the start been marked for citizenship in the kingdom of the gods.

The Greeks were much given to the custom of expressing appreciation for various forms of service rendered to mankind and to society by conspicuous individuals. This appreciation commonly took the form of a shrine erected to the memory of the departed and the observance of rites that virtually amounted to worship. Herodotus tells us that the Spartans esteemed so highly the blessings conferred upon them by their lawgiver Lycurgus that after his death they erected a temple in his honor. Also their distinguished general Lysander was said by Plutarch to have been the first person among the Greeks to whom cities raised altars as to a god and offered sacrifices. Athletes of exceptional prowess, like Euthymus, who expelled the demon from the town of Temesa, and the famous Theagenes, were similarly honored. There were many places, not only in Greece but in foreign lands, containing images of Theagenes, who was highly honored particularly for his reputed ability to heal diseases. The physician Hippocrates was rewarded for his skill in medicine by receiving divine honors like those which the Greeks paid to Hercules.[1]

Poets were honored with altars erected to their memory and with stated sacrifices. Homer was worshiped at various places,

---

[1] See Herodotus *History* i. 65; Plutarch *Lysander* xviii; Pausanias *Itinerary* vi. 11. 9; Pliny *Natural History* vii. 37.

even at distant Alexandria. Smyrna was particularly zealous in claiming to have been his birthplace, and it dedicated a temple in his honor. The citizens of Borysthenes on the north shore of the Black Sea were said to have made a god of Homer and a near-god of Achilles. At Delphi the Pythian priestess commanded the people to give the poet Pindar an equal share in all the first-fruits offered to Apollo.[2]

Philosophers enjoyed a like distinction. Aristotle is said to have erected an altar to Plato and later was himself similarly honored by his native city of Stagira. By the first century B.C. it had become the custom among some philosophers to make a deity of Plato, and even Lucretius could with difficulty resist the temptation to hail the revered founder of the Epicurean school as himself a god. It is less surprising that the disciples of Pythagoras should have converted the house of the philosopher into a temple where he was worshiped in consequence of the people's admiration for his character.

The Greeks also recognized a distinct class of person called "hero." In Hesiod's catalogue of successive ages, the fourth had been one when the earth was populated by men of heroic mold worthy of the name of demigods. They were the characters of Homeric story who had fought on the plains of Troy or before seven-gated Thebes. Long ago they had all passed from earth to the Elysian Fields set apart for their special enjoyment. There the fertile soil produced for them three times every year its honey-sweet fruits. These epic heroes included Achilles, Agamemnon, Menelaus, Hector, Theseus, and a multitude of others who were revered and worshiped.

---

[2] Strabo *Geography* xiv. 1. 37; Dio Chrysostom *Oration* xiv; Pausanias *Itinerary* ix. 23. 2.

Many heroes were reputed to have rendered mankind divine assistance as founders of cities, noble kings, or great warriors. At public expense cities often erected altars to their memory and celebrated religious rites in their honor. These customs survived far into Roman times.

Among well-remembered historical persons, Alexander the Great was the chief of heroes. He was much praised for the blessings he was presumed to have bestowed on mankind by forcing Greek culture on the crude barbarians. He was conscious of being divinely equipped to mollify the customs of crude peoples and to act as an arbiter of all nations. Those whom he could not peaceably persuade he compelled by force to submit to his rule, and this was done for the common good of humanity. Had not Alexander conquered the barbarians, they would have remained ignorant of Homer and Plato and would never have lived in glorious cities like Alexandria. In short, they would have remained uncivilized had not heaven intervened to bless the world by giving it a divine conquering savior.

The uncanny success of Alexander seemed to attest his supernatural personality even during his lifetime. The kings whom he had conquered so masterfully had themselves been worshiped as gods by their subjects. Must not their victor be an even greater god? His successors, particularly the Seleucids and the Ptolemies, carried on the tradition of the divine king, even though history provided no such magnificent demonstration of their ability to benefit mankind. They claimed to be epiphanies of deity—gods manifest in the flesh—and so ruled by divine right.

The Romans followed the example of the Greeks in deify-ing persons who had wrought nobly for the welfare of their contemporaries. The spokesmen brought forward in Cicero's dialogue on the nature of the gods represent different schools of thought, but they all take for granted that the Romans are familiar with the custom of paying divine honors to historical persons who have gained distinction for their service to mankind and society. The Epicurean speaks rather sarcastically of these individuals who have been recently admitted to the ancient body of the gods; they are, he says, the "gods of the illiterate."

Outside of Epicurean circles deification was thought to be an entirely fitting reward for those who had chosen to live for the help, the protection, and the preservation of their fellows. Hercules was the notable example. He had gone to heaven as the reward of virtue, and that honor never would have been won by him had he not during his stay among men paved his own way to glory. In Cicero's treatise on the laws much emphasis was placed on the propriety of worshiping the older heroes like Hercules and Romulus and also abstract deities representative of such virtues as valor, piety, fidelity, and intelligence. Since it was thought fitting that temples should be consecrated in their honor, men who had exemplified these virtues to an exceptional degree in their own lives deserved a similar reward. In Scipio's dream this conviction was affirmed: "A certain place in heaven is assigned to all who have preserved or assisted or improved their country, and they are to enjoy an endless duration of happiness."[3]

The deification of Romulus, the idealized founder of Rome,

[3] Cicero *Republic* vi. 13.

was well-nigh universally conceded.[4] And at an early date Julius Caesar was similarly honored. The magnitude of his accomplishments was heightened by contrast with his untimely end. While Caesar still lived, Romans feared his power, but, when death removed the menace, admiration for his accomplishments quickly blossomed into heroic deification. Even his surviving contemporaries could declare him worthy of this honor on account of his great achievements in the conquest of Gaul. In the next century there was no hesitation about giving him a place beside the divine Alexander.[5]

The peace which came to the Roman world with the establishment of the Empire by Augustus, and the long continuance of his regime, inspired the recognition of a new hero in the person of the emperor. Even during his lifetime his subjects were not slow to concede him this distinction. No one will take too seriously the compliments that Vergil and Horace were wont to pay to their imperial overlord, but one can be quite sure that they were not the only persons in the Empire to imagine that the beneficent regime of Augustus had been made possible through the presence of a very unusual man in office. The service he had rendered seemed to justify belief in his divinity.

In the East, where appreciation of rulers more readily expressed itself in the imagery of deification, the language of the Priene inscription was not at all extraordinary. It was quite fitting to call the emperor the common good of all men and

---

[4] E.g., Cicero *Tusculan* i. 12; *Nature of the Gods* iii. 15; *Laws* ii. 8; *Commonwealth* ii. 10; Dionysius of Halicarnassus *History* ii. 63; Livy *History* i. 16; Florus *History* i. 1; Tacitus *Annals* iv. 38; Plutarch *Romulus* xxviii; *Numa* ii; Ovid *Fasti* ii. 479 ff.

[5] Appian *Civil Wars* ii. 149 and 151.

to hail his birthday as the beginning of a new age for the world. By that event heaven had adorned life "most perfectly by granting us Augustus whom Providence filled with virtue for the benefit of mankind, sending him to be a savior for us as well as for our descendants, bringing all wars to an end and setting up all things in order." His subjects regarded it a privilege to be able to call him "savior and benefactor" and, indeed, "savior and god," "son of god," and "god Augustus, overseer of every land and sea."

When Augustus died, exaltation to heaven was his inevitable destiny, just as it had been the reward of Alexander the Great. Although Suetonius is hopelessly credulous, there is no reason to suppose that he did not represent the popular opinion of his day. He affirmed it to be common belief that even the soul of Julius Caesar had risen to heaven and was there to be seen in the form of a comet blazing in the sky for seven days during the first games that Augustus celebrated in honor of his martyred predecessor. The glorification of Augustus was still more apparent. A man of pretorian rank had declared under oath that he saw the spirit of Augustus ascend from the funeral pyre to heaven. Later writers felt the propriety of adding that this ascension had happened after the same manner in which the ascent of Romulus had been attested by the eyewitness Proculus. Thus Augustus, the latest savior of the Roman people, had gone to heaven to receive a suitable reward for his services to humanity.

II

The interest attaching to the earthly activity of the heroic savior varied widely in different settings, and the display of supernatural power in connection with his life on earth showed itself in a variety of manifestations. Sometimes this period of his existence was only a prelude to his apotheosis, when as a heaven-exalted divinity he became truly significant for mankind. In other instances a good deal of attention was paid to the events connected with his earthly career. If he was assumed to have been of strictly human ancestry, the element of supernaturalism showed itself in his wonderful accomplishments effected through the special favor of heaven or in his native ability to perform superhuman feats. Even the more legendary demigods were subjected to the same pragmatic tests.

Euripides, with his rationalistic leanings, had called Demeter and Dionysus the two chief deities of Greece because they were the gods of bread and wine. Diodorus, who filled his pages with uncritical rehearsals of current tradition, declared that among all the deities Dionysus and Demeter were most deserving of reverence because their benefits to the human race had been the greatest. The one had discovered the most pleasant drink and the other the most strengthening food. Also Dionysus was credited with having traveled all over the world to teach people the blessings of agriculture. Even the distant land of Egypt had received his ministrations. And, because Greeks and barbarians alike had shared his favor, all mankind rendered him immortal honors. Evidently the picture of Dionysus was now modeled after the likeness of the divine Alexander.

The Egyptian divinities, Isis and Osiris, were portrayed in similar imagery. Their title to worship was based on the wonderful benefits they had conferred upon humanity during their period of residence on earth. Osiris had traveled over the whole world, acquainting crude peoples with the amenities of civilization. Isis also had spent her time in the exact administration of justice and had surpassed all other rulers in bestowing blessings on her subjects. Not the least of her distinctions had been skill in finding out medicines for the recovery of men's health. She was believed to have had ability even to raise the dead and by this means had made her son Horus immortal. Consequently, both she and Osiris after their death were numbered among the gods and rightfully received honors equal to those which had been accorded even the greatest of the deities.

Another hero much revered for his therapeutic activity was the Greek Asklepios, called Aesculapius by the Romans. In Homeric story he was a physician in the service of the Greek army, but long before the beginning of Christian times a wealth of legend had gathered around his name. While on earth he had displayed marvelous ability to heal diseases and had even restored the dead to life. By this act he had incurred the anger of Zeus, who, fearing lest mortals would escape their divinely decreed destiny, hurled a thunderbolt at Asklepios. But the great healer could not be cheated out of his proper reward. Through the intervention of Apollo, Zeus was persuaded to place Asklepios among the stars. But the reality of his earthly career was not forgotten. He was credited with the invention of probes, bandages, purgatives, and dental instruments. Several places contended for the honor of showing his tomb, and at each he was duly worshiped.

Among the reputed benefactors of humanity, Hercules enjoyed especial honor. He had been compelled to labor hardest to win immortality. Like the Jesus of Christian tradition, Hercules had withstood the tempter before entering on his lifework. On arriving at manhood, he had been approached by two figures personifying virtue and vice, who appeared to him in a vision as he sat alone in a solitary place. Vice offered him a life of ease and pleasure, while virtue invited him to undertake hardships in the service of others. Hercules chose the thorny pathway, and the gods allotted him such toils as no one before had ever endured. But he successfully performed one feat after another, his crowning accomplishment being a descent to the lower world and a safe return. There he had delivered from their torment the afflicted Theseus and Ascalaphus and had overcome barehanded the three-headed monster that kept guard over the gates of hell. So mighty a hero fittingly immolated himself on Mount Oeta and was caught up from the funeral pyre in a cloud to Olympus. Euripides was versifying popular belief when he wrote of Hercules:

> He hath burst from earth's dungeons, hath rifted the chain
>   Of Pluto's deep prison!
> Thou art worthier to rule than the churl-king slain,
>   O my King rearisen![6]

Hercules' fame as a victor over the power of death was known far beyond Greece. His "awakening" or "arising"— the Greek expression is the same as that used for the notion of resurrection, whether of Jesus or of others in the New Testament—was celebrated at various places. The Jewish historian Josephus states, on the authority of a certain Menander who had translated the Phoenician records into Greek, that Solo-

---

[6] *Madness of Hercules*, trans. A. S. Way, ll. 187 ff.

mon's friend King Hiram of Tyre had built a temple to Hercules and had instituted the ceremonies of his arising. Presumably the arising was from a funeral pyre prepared for the occasion. In Tarsus, Paul's native city, a similar ceremony was still observed at the beginning of the second century A.D. The people of Tarsus counted Hercules to be the founder of their city and honored him with a very handsome funeral pyre.[7]

Great heroes like Hercules and Dionysus, and others of lesser distinction, commanded the faith of people all about the Mediterranean in imperial times. They were trusted, not only because of the reality of their historic careers attested by alleged tombs shown at many places, but because in the art and theology of the cults one learned of the heroes' triumph over death and ascension to the sky. In the first century B.C., Cicero could remark that one needed only to examine the sepulchers shown in Greece and to recall, if one had been initiated in the mysteries, the teachings inculcated in these ceremonies, in order to perceive how extensively men believed in gods who had been raised from the dead and exalted to heaven.

The picture of a triumph over death was a conspicuous feature in those widely popular and highly revered mysteries connected with the name of the great mother-goddess Demeter and her daughter Kore (Persephone). Tradition told of the mother's grief when her daughter was carried off to the lower world by Pluto, the king of the nether regions. In her bereavement the mother refused to nourish the life of nature, and only when Kore was restored to her did dormant vegetation revive. Even though it was decreed that the daughter must

---

[7] Josephus *Antiquities* viii. 5. 3; Dio Chrysostom *Oration* xxxiii. 47.

spend part of each year in the lower world, the assurance that after the death of winter her return would guarantee nature's resurrection signified a perpetually recurring triumph of life over death. It is not surprising that the goddess who thus successfully completed her yearly pilgrimage to Hades and back to earth, thereby insuring the preservation of life in this world and a kindly reception for her devotees when they too descended to the abodes of the dead, should have been gratefully designated "Savior Kore" at different places in Greece.

Dionysus (Bacchus) was conspicuously a dying and rising god among the Greeks. He was widely famed not only for deeds performed during his earthly career but also for his significant victory over death. The tomb of Dionysus was shown at Delphi beside the oracle of Apollo, and the sepulcher is said to have borne the inscription: "Dionysus the son of Semele lies buried here." Here his awakening in the springtime was celebrated with sacred rites. Plutarch addressed his treatise on the Isis mysteries to a certain Clea, who had herself headed the Bacchanalian rites at Delphi, where the devotees, driven by divine frenzy, raised loud shouts and went through strange motions in honor of the god. Also they conducted a secret service in the temple of Apollo the function of which was to wake up the sleeping Bacchus.

Orpheus, in many respects the double of Dionysus, was widely reputed in tradition to have suffered a violent death after which he ascended to heaven. When Pausanias was sight-seeing in Greece, he was told various stories about this hero's death. The honor of possessing his mortal remains was claimed by different places where his tomb could be seen, and the urn containing his bones was sometimes shown as a sacred relic. Once a shepherd lying down on the hero's grave at noonday was so filled with the vitality of the deceased that he broke out into beautiful music while he slept.

Outside of Greece the dying and reviving divinity was a very conspicuous figure. The Syrian Adonis was popularly worshiped with rites of lamentation and rejoicing to celebrate his death and rising again to life. His grave was to be seen in a cavern of the rock at Ghineh near Byblos. Above it was a carving depicting Adonis in conflict with the wild boar by which he was slain, while Aphrodite is shown mourning for the deceased. There were variant traditions regarding the manner of his death, but they all agreed in representing that the youthful god had died by violence and had been loudly lamented by grieving women, whose sorrow was presently turned into joy by Adonis' restoration to life.

Although Byblos in Syria was the principal seat of Adonis' worship, the popularity of the cult at Alexandria as early as the beginning of the third century B.C. is attested by Theocritus' poem on the festival of Adonis. The poet draws a vivacious picture of the preparation for this feast in the palace of Ptolemy II and vividly portrays the acclamations and excitement connected with the celebration. This Easter song depicts a holy marriage between Adonis and Aphrodite interrupted by the death of the bridegroom. Loud wailing attends this calamity, but the agony of the funeral service is quickly relieved by the anticipation of Adonis' return to life. He is hailed as the one who, above all others, has power to journey back and forth between the nether regions and the world of mankind. In this he is said to transcend in ability even the greatest of the Greek heroes, a claim that the devotees of other similar cults would scarcely admit.

The mysteries of Adonis were still popular in the second century A.D., when Lucian visited Byblos and participated in the ceremonies which he described in his treatise on the Syrian goddess. The annual festival was celebrated in the springtime. At that time the neighboring stream, swollen by the melting snow from the Lebanon Mountains, brought down to the sea large quantities of red mud which made the waters seem colored by blood. The faithful called it the blood of Adonis shed in his conflict with a wild boar. Then it was that his devotees "beat their breasts and wail every year and perform their secret ritual and make signs of mourning through the whole countryside. When they have finished their mourning and wailing they sacrifice in the first place to Adonis as to one who has departed this life. After this, they allege that he is alive again and exhibit his effigy in the sky."[8]

Very similar rites were celebrated in honor of the Phrygian Attis, whose cult was closely associated with that of the great mother of the gods, Cybele. One tradition represented that he had died in conflict with a wild beast, while another reported that he had sacrificed his own life. But, in either event, mourning for his demise was a conspicuous item in the cult. The grief of Cybele, Attis lying dead in his coffin, and his restoration to life were vividly depicted in the art of the cult and may be seen today in many archeological remains. In the time of the emperor Claudius (A.D. 41–54) the rites of Attis were elaborately celebrated at Rome. The principal features of this great drama were, first, the felling of a pine tree sacred

---

[8] Lucian *Syrian Goddess* vi.

to Attis, a rite typifying the death of the divinity. This symbol of the god was swathed in graveclothes and treated like a corpse to represent the dead Attis. On the following day the devotees abstained from food and mourned the decease of the deity. Following the funeral ceremony, the initiates kept their mysterious vigil, which was supposed to confer on the mystic the life of a new Attis. Then suddenly sadness turned to joy; the god arose from his sleep in death, and his followers gave vent to great jubilation.

Egypt gave the ancient world the very old and widely popular hero-divinity, Osiris. He, too, had died in conflict with a hostile power. The goddess Isis, with whom his name is closely associated, was overcome with grief. There is a luxuriant growth of legend connected with his death and her suffering. But ultimately both she and the slain Osiris came off victorious over their enemies and attained to a position of superior authority in the realm of the supernatural. Their worshipers, who were to be found widely scattered about the Mediterranean world at the beginning of the Christian Era, reverenced these Egyptian divinities particularly for the assurance which they gave of a blessed immortality.

Probably Plutarch's treatise on *Isis and Osiris* was an accurate summary of popular feeling toward these divinities throughout large areas of the Roman Empire in the first century A.D. Undoubtedly he expressed common opinion when he said that the efforts of Isis ceased not with her own struggle to satisfy her quest for the recovery of her slaughtered brother but were a perpetual benefit to humanity because of the sacred ceremonies which had been established in consequence of her activities. Isis had "consecrated at one and the same time both lessons of piety and consolation in suffering for men and women when overtaken by misfortune, and she, together with Osiris, having been translated from the rank of good demons up to that of gods .... received not inappropriately the united honors of gods and demons everywhere, both in the regions above the earth and in those underground, possessing the supreme power." Paul claimed the same distinction for his risen Christ (Phil. 2:9–11).

Last of all, Persia made its contribution toward the imagery of the heroic savior. The religion of Mithra was a vigorous rival of Christianity during the second and third centuries. The central figure in this cult was a glorious hero who while on earth had participated in many gigantic conflicts. But ultimately he passed victoriously from earth to heaven, where he faithfully watched over his followers. Since Mithraic religion was much concerned about the struggle between good and evil in the world, Mithra devoted himself to the ideals of deliverance and redemption. Pictured as a figure miraculously born from a rock, he burst upon the world with redeeming light like that of the sun itself. He and his heroic associates brought their earthly career to an end in a last supper that was commemorated by disciples in memory of his triumph. At last he would return to earth to raise the dead and annihilate all the forces of evil. In the meantime from his position among the immortals he continued to mediate supernatural help to his devotees.

III

The supernatural credentials of the heroic savior were found not alone in the memory of his earthly service to humanity, or even in the fact of his exaltation to heaven after death. He was also provided with appropriate supernatural antecedents. Pindar had explained the genesis of distinguished individuals on the theory that they were reincarnations of souls who, after nine years of incarceration in Hades, had won their release from Persephone, the goddess of the lower world. When their atonement had been thus accomplished, they were permitted to return to earth. Persons who possessed these souls became "illustrious kings and men swift in strength and superior in wisdom and therefore they are called holy heroes among men."[9]

To explain the hero by giving him a soul superior to that of the average man was a notion adopted by Plato, from whom it passed on to the Romans. In its Latin form the doctrine was promulgated by Vergil in describing the experiences of Aeneas on a visit to the lower world. There he was shown pre-existent spirits who, when they return to their "allotted place in life," will distinguish themselves in public affairs and make the Roman world glorious. Conspicuous among these persons were Romulus and Augustus.[10]

In later times when Christians were endeavoring to explain the distinctiveness of Jesus on the theory of a pre-existent divine Logos incarnate in his earthly manifestation, heathen theologians were still advocating the old doctrine of pre-existent souls. One of the Hermetic treatises represented Isis giving instruction to her son Horus on this important theme. When Horus asked how it came about that kingly souls appeared on earth, his mother replied that the king is a creation

[9] Pindar *Threnoi* Frag. 133 (Schroeder).

[10] Plato *Meno* 81; Vergil *Aeneid* vi. 756 ff.

of the gods, who send down to earth a superior soul destined for this noble calling. The king is least among the gods but first among mortals. While upon earth he is not a full deity, yet he is to be distinguished from other mortals by the godlike element resident in his person.

While philosophers were struggling with the problem of pre-existence, the man on the street depicted in more picturesque fashion the supernatural credentials of the heroes in whom he trusted. Evidences of divinity were thought to be more readily perceivable in the miraculous displays connected with the earthly career of a hero. It was not so easy for the common man to discover the superior excellence of an incarnate soul as it was to convince himself that he had witnessed a miracle or to imagine that such deeds had been seen by others. For people of this temper and with these limitations legend was a far better instrument than philosophy for accrediting heroic saviors.

All the great heroes of tradition had performed wonderful deeds. These displays might very properly occur with no other motive than that of attesting the supernatural ability of the performer. It was commonly believed in the Roman Empire that the gods accredited their favorites by special displays of miraculous power. Such exhibitions were an evidence that the person so favored had been appointed by heaven to mediate divine assistance to his contemporaries. In presenting Jesus to gentile readers, the authors of the several New Testament gospels recognized the importance of exhibiting him in the role of a mighty miracle-worker, if he were to compete successfully with rival heroes who already held the field.

A story of supernatural birth was a particularly favorite

way of accrediting heroic saviors. Sometimes the word "hero" was said to be derived from *eros,* meaning love. Heroes, therefore, were demigods born of the love of a god for a mortal woman or of a mortal man for a goddess. Just as the Jews read in their Bible that divinities mingling with the daughters of men had produced a race of giants (Gen. 6:1–4), so the Greeks in their Homeric scriptures were told that Poseidon had visited a certain earthly woman, admonishing her to be glad in their love, for, when the year comes round, "thou shalt give birth to glorious children, for not weak are the embraces of the gods." And in due time she bore Pelias and Neleus, who grew to be "mighty men, servants of Zeus."

Hercules was reputed to be the son of Zeus. His mother was Alcmene, herself well descended among mortal women and so virtuous that Zeus knew it would be impossible to seduce her. Therefore, he assumed the form of her husband in order to produce from her a divine child. Popular reverence for Hercules demanded that both the mother and the god should have been prompted by the sincerest of motives in begetting their noble son. Again it is Diodorus who is the convenient spokesman of popular opinion in the Augustan age. He writes that, when Zeus visited Alcmene, he "tripled the length of the night, and by the amount of time spent in the procreation of the child signified beforehand the superior strength of his progeny."

Another son of Zeus was Dionysus, and his mother Semele was hailed as one who "gave birth to a god." Euripides had used the expression *theon tekein,* the prototype of the later Christian title *theotokos,* applied to the mother of Jesus. The twin brothers Castor and Pollux, much beloved for their interest in the welfare of mariners, were also illustrious sons of Zeus. They had been born to be the "saviors of mortals" and of their frail barks when driven before the winds of winter on a pitiless sea. But these sons of deity, it must be remembered, were particularly insistent upon righteous conduct. They refused to help those who worked abominations, but to him who loved faith and righteousness they brought salvation from all distress.

Asklepios, beloved for his healing ministrations, was believed to have been a son of the god Apollo. It was in the land of Epidaurus, which contained his celebrated sanctuary, that his mother had given him birth. Although she exposed the babe, he was presently discovered by a shepherd who immediately recognized that the brilliant light shining from the infant's face indicated that the hand of a god was manifest in the occurrence. Quickly the fame of the child spread abroad over every land and sea, as one having all power to heal the sick and even to raise the dead.

Belief in the supernatural ancestry of famous historical persons like Alexander the Great was inevitable in a world in which divine generation was so popularly accepted to explain the genesis of heroic saviors. Even had not the theory of divine parentage for oriental and Egyptian kings already existed, the Greek imagination might easily have devised for Alexander a similar tradition. It was only appropriate that Zeus, the chief of the gods, should have been the father of Alexander, the greatest of princes. Neither the skepticism of Livy nor the ridicule of Lucian could shake the popular faith in the divine descent of this mighty hero.

The less imaginative Romans were nonetheless ready to ascribe divine parentage to their kings and great men. Romulus was commonly believed to have been the son of the god Mars and the virgin priestess Rhea Silvia. A still better-known historical character, Scipio Africanus, like Alexander, was rumored to have been a man of divine extraction. The tradition is said to have arisen from his custom of visiting the Capitoline Temple of Jupiter for a period of meditation and quiet before transacting any business, either of a public or of a private nature. Also, Pompey seems to have tried to increase his prestige during the period of the civil wars by making out, on the strength of two successful naval encounters, that he was the son of Poseidon.

Augustus and his successors in the imperial office could hardly have escaped, even had they so desired, the ascription to them of a supernatural origin. Before Augustus had been established in power, Vergil had embodied in his fourth *Eclogue* the popular belief that it was Rome's destiny to be ruled by a child born under the special favor of heaven. And once the regime of Augustus had become firmly established, it was not difficult to see in his person the fulfilment of this heathen messianic hope. Apollo, it was said, had been his father. Suetonius narrated an incident found in older records describing the manner in which the god had visited Augustus' mother, and how both the father and the mother before the birth of the child had been marvelously instructed by visions and dreams.

Sometimes even philosophers did not escape the doubtful honor of alleged divine parentage. Plato's nephew, Speusippus, so the story goes, had sponsored the tradition that his uncle was a son of Apollo, who warned the husband of the mother not to approach her until the divine child had been born. Literal divine parenthood was not, however, a generally accepted mode of thinking in philosophical circles. The Stoic could say that the wise man is a "son of god," using the expression with reference not to a physical generation but to an especial endowment of Logos resident in the individual's personality. The disciples of Pythagoras knew a story that made him a son of Hermes, but this was not universally believed. The Pythagoreans were hesitant about locating the superiority of any person in the realm of the flesh, yet they believed that the wisdom of Pythagoras was superhuman because he had a divine soul sent to mankind from the realm of Apollo. This belief seemed to be substantiated by the tradition that Pythagoras had been born of a virgin and had shown himself master of all kinds of wisdom.

Among the intellectual men of the Roman Empire in the early centuries of the Christian Era, the propriety of supposing that the seed of divinity could mix with mortals seems to have been seriously discussed. While Plutarch thought it quite proper to call Apollo the father of Plato, he knew others who said that it was repugnant to the incorruptibility of the deity to be concerned with the generation of mortals. But Plutarch himself was convinced that there was no impropriety in assuming that deity might visit women who were wise and pure. Plutarch was ready to adopt the opinion of the Egyptians, whom he cited to the effect that one must not suppose that a god in person had intercourse with a mortal woman, but that the act was accomplished through the agency of a "spirit of god."[11]

Thus it had come about that, from the philosopher in his lecture hall to the most illiterate man on the street, the gentile world exalted the notion of divine ancestry in one form or another as a most desirable credential attesting the supernatural power of many heroic saviors.

IV

When the name of Jesus was first introduced among Gentiles, he was portrayed in the role of a distinctively Jewish type of heroic savior. By arising from the dead and ascending to heaven, he had become the Messiah who would return at an early date to establish his supernatural kingdom and execute judgment on all sinners. Palestine was to be the scene of the event and Jews were to be its chief beneficiaries. Thus would be realized the long-deferred Jewish hope for the advent of the messianic deliverer who would rescue the descendants of Abraham from their oppressors. But this portrayal of a coming deliverer did not make a wide appeal to contemporary Jews, and relatively few of them joined the Christian movement.

On the other hand, Gentiles showed greater readiness to attach themselves to the new movement and to find in its heroic figure satisfaction for their needs. As early as the year 50 Christianity had become a vigorous gentile propaganda, and from this time on there was a continually growing inter-

---

[11] *Numa* iv; *Symposiacs* vii. 1. 3. In Plutarch the generative agent was "spirit of god" (*pneuma theou*), and in Matt. 1:20 and Luke 1:35 it was "holy spirit" (*pneuma hagion*), but the gospel child was a "son of God."

est in presenting Jesus as a savior for every man in the Roman world regardless of his racial ancestry. Paul never wearied of insisting that faith in Jesus as the hero who had died, arisen from the dead, and ascended to heaven, whence he would presently descend to officiate at the judgment of all mankind, was the only hope of salvation for every man, both Jew and Gentile.

A belief that salvation was to be attained through trust in the accomplishment of a deceased historical individual, later apotheosized as a reward for his self-sacrificing service to humanity, sounds strange on the lips of Paul, who boasted of his competence in the Jewish religion of his youth. Certainly he found nothing there to suggest that salvation was to be attained through the death of a man who would subsequently be elevated to the dignity of a god. He persuaded himself that he could find ample warrant in the Hebrew Scriptures for his new faith, but on that point he was radically at variance with the vast majority of his fellow-Israelites. Gentiles, however, were much better prepared by their traditions to give his message a favorable reception. They were accustomed to look for help to heroic saviors of a similar type, and they were quite ready to hear the testimonials that could be offered on behalf of the new savior.

Paul had said comparatively little about the heroic features of Jesus' life on earth, except to call attention to the manner of his death and his subsequent elevation to heaven. But other Christians gave greater attention to the display of redemptive powers by Jesus during his earthly career. The author of Acts provided his gentile patron, Theophilus, with an epitome of missionary preaching put into the mouth of Peter, according to which the heroic elements in the life of the historical Jesus began to show themselves from the moment of his baptism. On that occasion God had anointed him with the Holy Spirit and with power. Immediately Jesus began traveling about to perform a saving work by healing the sick and driving demons out of all who were possessed. If Theophilus had been accustomed to hear of the beneficent labors of a Hercules or a Dionysus or an Asklepios, he now had an opportunity to learn of one who had shown himself still more effective in performing beneficial service for mankind. And, like other heroes, Jesus had triumphed over death and been elevated to the heavens (Acts 10:38–43).

Each Gospel writer devoted himself extensively to the heroic activity of the historical Jesus. He taught mankind supernatural wisdom, he healed sick bodies by his divine power, and his word of command struck terror into the hearts of evil demons. Some of the evangelists were able to furnish additional evidence of his claim to attention. In Matthew and Luke readers were told of supernatural displays connected with the announcement of his birth. To a Gentile familiar with saviors accredited by divine parentage, Jesus, born of a mother who had been impregnated by the Holy Spirit, might now readily seem to be a formidable rival of all other heroic saviors. A reader of the Fourth Gospel would learn further that Christianity's hero was not only an incarnate god but that while on earth he had made every possible effort to display among men the glory which he had with the Father before the foundation of the world. One who shared characteristic philosophical shyness toward the notion of literal divine parentage for the hero's flesh could believe when reading the

Gospel of John that Jesus had been distinctive because he was an incarnation of the divine Logos (Word), while physically he had been a true son of Joseph. His uniqueness lay entirely in the realm of the spirit; he was truly a god manifest in genuinely human flesh.

Before the close of the first century Jesus had been presented to the Gentiles in a fairly complete heroic role. In the opinion of his disciples he was not simply another divine helper to be trusted for some special type of service but was the one all-sufficient redeemer who supplanted all rivals. Christians vigorously affirmed that there was no other name under heaven known to mankind by which one could obtain genuine salvation. And since he tolerated no rivals and no associates, it was necessary that his disciples demonstrate his ability to render the full quota of services that had previously been credited to his predecessors.

In this endeavor Christians ultimately proved successful. But, difficult as their task may at first have seemed, they had no need to teach Gentiles for the first time the desirability of trusting in heroic redeemers equipped with divine power to render supernatural assistance to needy humanity. The more exacting task of the Christian preacher had been to transform the rather forbidding imagery of a Jewish Messiah, presently to institute a terrible day of judgment, into the more friendly and elaborately adorned figure of a gentile savior who had mediated divine help to mankind during his earthly career and who now from his position of power in the heavens insured both a present and a future salvation for his devotees.

CHAPTER V

THE HUMAN APPROACH
TO THE GODS

THERE was a great wealth of divine help available for men living in the ancient world. But the supernatural powers had to be properly approached, firmly laid hold upon, and effectively harnessed in the service of a seeking humanity. For many centuries prior to the Christian Era the various people around the Mediterranean basin had industriously devoted themselves to the task of building up an adequate machinery for man's use in dealing with the gods. Business with the supernatural was conducted on a large scale and with great energy. The Christian movement was able to learn from its heathen competitors many a lesson in the organization and technique necessary for an effective approach to the sources of superhuman help universally assumed to be available for mankind.

I

The Gentiles were very diligent in rendering worship to their deities. Christians commented on this fact, although they thought the procedure to be wholly senseless and demonic. Yet they half-admired the exemplary fidelity with which the heathen every day on arising from his sleep rushed to worship his idols. He sometimes traveled long distances to attend services and undertook no kind of work without first

consulting the deities. In the centuries following the establishment of the Empire by Augustus, a traveler in any part of the
Roman world found himself confronted on every hand by a
great variety of different cults. People of all classes were
zealous suppliants of one and sometimes of several divinities.

The faithful worship of the gods was advocated by many a
gentile preacher. The Greeks had been taught that every man
should offer sacrifice according to his ability, approaching the
deities in a holy and a pure manner. Suitable burnt offerings
and propitiatory libations were to be rendered at the proper
seasons. In the evening before one went to sleep incense was to
be burned, and again in the morning when the holy light of
day brought back new life to mankind. Homer could be cited
in support of the belief that men when they had sinned might
avert the wrath of heaven by prayers and sacrifices, by libations and the savory odor of burnt offerings.[1] In a spirit that
suggests the temper of the Hebrew prophets, Hesiod had admonished the Greeks to perform faithfully customary religious
rites in order that the gods "may entertain towards thee a
propitious heart and spirit, that thou mayest buy the land of
others and not others thine."[2]

Admirers of Socrates made him a model religious person.
He was always conducting himself most piously in accordance
with the laws of his country, particularly in matters of religion. He prayed earnestly to the gods, but he always left it
to them to answer his requests according to their own knowledge of what was best. Their will, not his, should prevail. He
sacrificed as elaborately as his circumstances would permit,

[1] *Iliad* ix. 493.

[2] *Works and Days* 335 ff.

believing that the gods took greater pleasure in the meager offerings of the devout man than in the more abundant gifts of the less pious rich. Most important of all, in whatever manner the gods indicated their will to Socrates, he is said to have obeyed absolutely the behests of the deities. He also taught that man should appeal to the gods not only in critical moments but in all the affairs of life. If the farmer desired a successful year, he should supplicate the gods for a good harvest, for increase of his flocks, for the warding-off of disease from horses and sheep and cattle, and for protection from all other dangers threatening his crops and his stock. The Greeks recognized the desirability of calling on the gods to safeguard all the concerns of one's life.[3]

The Romans were even more noted than the Greeks for diligence in sacred things. Already in the second century B.C. a Greek observer, who thought himself exceptionally free from superstition, remarked upon the devotion of the Romans. They were commended for their scrupulous fear of the gods and were said to have made pious considerations supreme both in private and in public business. The Romans themselves admitted that conspicuous examples of impiety had not been wanting even in positions of great responsibility during the course of their history, but neglect of sacred ceremonies had always proved a sure forerunner of disaster, while assiduous observance of religious rites had always been rewarded with success. The pious man could say without fear of contradiction that everyone knew the city of Rome had been built by auspices and that all things had been conducted by auspices during war and peace both at home and abroad. The gods, it

---

[3] Xenophon *Memorabilia* i. 3. 1–4; *Economics* v. 19.

was said, are most deserving of respect from the human race, for they observe what sort of person one is, how he acts, what designs he entertains, and with what motives and sincerity he performs religious rites, and they take account of both the righteous and the wicked.[4]

In the imperial age, when the religions native to Greece and Italy were being extensively supplemented by the rapid expansion of foreign cults from Asia and Egypt, the importance of worship, both for the life of the individual and for the welfare of the state, received further emphasis. Time and again, in critical periods both private citizens and the government showed great concern regarding the matter of adequate divine protection. On different occasions the worship of new gods had been introduced into Rome as a means of giving renewed energy to the failing power of the state. While it is true that, in general, foreign religions were accepted with reserve and strange rites were kept within bounds, there was a growing feeling among the Romans that in the past they had been able to derive no small measure of benefit from the adoption of new cults. Their ceremonies provided new ways of approaching the supernatural powers.

There were in antiquity persons of puritan temper who sought to prevent worship of the gods from degenerating into gross superstition. Plato had set the model for all philosophers in his treatise on the *Laws,* in which he had much to say about the way in which religion should be regulated in an ideal state. When a man wanted to worship, instead of setting up in his own house private religious ceremonies, he should take his

---

[4] Polybius *History* i. 505–6; Livy *History* vi. 41; Cicero *Nature of the Gods* i. 2; ii. 3; *Laws* ii. 7. 15.

sacrifices to the priests and priestesses, who know how properly to perform the rites. Only for purposes of prayer might private assemblies gather; the rites of worship on their more formal side were too sacred and important to be trusted to the ignorant masses.

Later philosophers among the Greeks and Romans followed the example of Plato in criticizing the superstitions of the ignorant, without, however, denying to the individual freedom to worship the gods according to the dictates of his conscience. Yet they strove to purify and elevate the conception of worship as they found it current among the masses of humanity. Cicero, like Socrates, insisted that purity of soul was necessary for an approach to the gods. He advocated that all costliness be banished from the temples and that men when they entered into the sanctuary, which they ought frequently to do, should keep the divine image before their eyes. Nor should they ever forget the fear of punishment awaiting offenders. The worshiper should remember that evil men could not propitiate the deity with gifts; the favor of heaven could not be bought; it could be secured only by a pure heart and sincere motives. While the gods were forgiving, Cicero was as emphatic as Paul in maintaining that sin should not be committed in order that grace might abound.[5]

The desirability of a sane and intelligent attitude in worship continued to be emphasized by thoughtful men among the Greeks and Romans all through the period when Christianity was slowly gaining ground in the Roman Empire. The deity was to be worshiped with the mind and the conscience fully

[5] Cicero's summary of the laws relating to worship should be read in their entirety (Laws ii. 8–9).

active during the ceremony. Fear, magic, and absurd practices ought to find no place in the life of the suppliant when approaching the gods. Persons who entertained these perverted ideas needed first to be educated by the philosopher in order to learn more truly wherein the realities of genuine religion consisted. Plutarch found a ready hearing among the intelligentsia when he alleged that much of the worship to be seen in connection with many contemporary cults was simply gross superstition. It might have been better had there been no gods at all than that there should be any who would accept such worship and take pleasure in such rites.[6]

The effort to refine worship in the fire of intellectualism was not carried so far by Plutarch, and those of like mind, as to advocate the abolition of traditional rites or the abandonment of popular religious notions. Worship was still the indispensable means by which suppliant humanity could hope to obtain a hearing with the deities. A century earlier Seneca had said, citing Aristotle as his authority, that the most reverent moment in a person's life was the hour of worship. The temple was to be entered with fitting gravity, the eyes were to be lowered and the toga to be drawn over the face, and every token of modesty to be exhibited when one approached the sacrifice. And Plutarch, severe as he was in his criticism of superstition, was equally antagonistic toward atheism. He could not tolerate the man who attended religious ceremonies with a sardonic grin on his face, who made light of what he saw there, and who scoffed at sacred things. For the reasonable man the festivals and banquets at the temples were pleasant and holy acts. Rites of initiation, the Dionysiac celebrations,

[6] Plutarch *Superstition* xii.

prayers to the deities and adorations of their images—all properly belonged to the program of the sensible worshiper.[7]

The masses of mankind felt less at ease in the presence of the supernatural powers, but they participated no less faithfully in religious ceremonies. They were wont to take the procedure so seriously that they turned pale when the garland was placed on their heads, and they prayed with faltering tongue. Overcome by awe before the altar, they offered their libations with a trembling hand. When the atmosphere of the place was heavy with odors of incense and perfume, the presence of the divine filled them with fear rather than with joy. So at least Plutarch interpreted the state of mind of those persons who were unable to entertain his intellectual attitude toward the act of worship. But whether the people whom he criticized had a false or a correct opinion about the nature of worship, one thing at least is clear. They were all suppliants before the gods. It was only the Epicureans, and they were comparatively few in number, who did not place their destinies on the knees of the gods.

While philosophers thought it desirable that all men should worship in a uniformly decorous manner, as a matter of fact society demanded a wide range of religious ceremonies to meet the needs of many different types of person mingling within the syncretistic life of that day. Different individuals chose to journey heavenward by different routes, and there was a sufficient variety of performances to permit every man a liberal choice of means by which the desired goal was thought to be attainable. Some of the rites were performed with a high display of enthusiasm, while others were celebrated without

[7] Seneca *Natural Questions* vii. 30; Plutarch *Superstition* ix.

any marked exhibition of emotion. Sometimes music was extensively employed to give vivacity to the worship, while at other times there was no music at all in connection with the rites. Some cults stressed the notion of the mysterious and performed their most sacred ceremonies in secret, while others were wide open to the public.

In every part of the Roman Empire one found an innumerable array of altars, sanctuaries, and temples that were visited by people both individually and in large groups for the celebration of either private or public religious acts. There was no city or countryside that did not have many sanctuaries. At the more noteworthy shrines people gathered in large numbers on great festive occasions. Annually swarms of pilgrims came from far and near to visit the holy place at Hierapolis explicitly described by Lucian in his treatise on the Syrian goddess. A similar popularity was enjoyed by the Dionysiac religious plays which in Lucian's day were yearly celebrated in Ionia and Pontus. People from the country round about would leave everything else and sit for whole days watching the ceremonies.

The older Greek gods, both in their original homes and in the cities to which they had migrated, were provided with many holidays on which hosts of people were found ready to participate in acts of worship. Roman, Asiatic, and Egyptian deities enjoyed similar honors both at home and in far-distant lands. Long before Christians took up the practice, Gentiles had been in the habit when on a journey of performing devotions at shrines by the wayside. It was the custom for people who were religiously inclined to halt at a grove or a sacred place to say a prayer, present an offering, and tarry for a sea-son. Even though bent on urgent business, this seemly respect for religion was not to be forgotten.[8]

In all the various types of worship the suppliant was provided with a more or less elaborate ritual. No matter what his status socially or culturally might be, the formalities of the cult enabled him to negotiate with the gods on behalf of any and every interest connected with his life. If he were a general leading an army into battle, or a prince contemplating some mighty enterprise affecting the destiny of empires, or if he were only a menial in the humblest household, he found available in one or another of the existing religions a well-tried and trusted machinery for ascertaining the divine will with reference to all his needs. Whatever the crisis in life might be, whether it was an affair of public business, a purely temporal and personal concern, or a matter of life and death, no one needed to suffer from ignorance of sacred rites necessary for performing one's duty toward the supernatural powers and for deriving therefrom the guidance and protection desired.

II

Prayer was one of the most common and effective instruments employed by men in their quest for divine assistance. While the philosopher might contend that gods could be trusted of their own accord to bless the pious and punish the wicked, it required only slight observation to note that this ideal principle was not always operative in real life. Everyone knew that frequently the good man suffered adversity while the wicked prospered. In his efforts to obtain the divine favor man himself had to take the initiative, and prayer was his

[8] Apuleius *Florida* i.

readiest instrument for this purpose. Gentiles as well as Christians believed in the propriety of importunate prayer (Luke 11:5–13). Indeed, not alone would neglect of prayer result in failure to receive such gifts as the gods might otherwise be able to bestow but it might be cause for offense on the part of the deity. Homer expressed this sentiment in poetic imagery when he called prayers the daughters of Zeus that bring great blessings to the man who shows them due respect; but if they are ruthlessly repelled, they mount up to the throne of god to become the accusers of men. The mere neglect of prayer would of itself invite the wrath of heaven.

The Greeks were notably a praying people. In both private and public concerns no important undertaking was launched without an initial appeal to heaven. Whether people convened in a court of justice, in a popular assembly, or in a public festivity, the ceremony opened with prayer. Even the orator contemplating a difficult situation sought divine help to give force and favor to his message. Demosthenes began his famous oration *On the Crown* by declaring that he prayed to every god and goddess for the good will of his hearers with the hope that deity would put it into their minds to yield him an attentive and respectful hearing. Similarly, Socrates, before departing from the place where he had been discoursing with his friends, tarried for a closing prayer addressed to "beloved Pan" and all other deities supposed to frequent the place. He prayed for beauty in the inward soul and harmony between the outward and the inner man, he would reckon the wise to be the wealthy, and he would have only such a quantity of gold as a temperate man could bear and carry.[9]

[9] Plato *Phaedrus* 279.

Prayer was a solemn performance. A correct ritual was important. The deity to be addressed was the one popularly believed to have a concern for those particular interests that bore most heavily upon the mind of the individual suppliant. One must come to terms with those divinities who were supposed to frequent the territory in which one resided. But in the event of a great crisis it might be necessary to journey to some more distant shrine to petition a god reputed to have under his special care the particular concern involved. In fact, the situation might be so perplexing that it was necessary to consult a seer or an oracle in order to ascertain the name of the divinity to whom a special type of appeal should be made, but the proper god was always to be found if man persisted with sufficient energy and patience in his quest.

Formal public prayer must often have been a very impressive performance. Thucydides describes such an occasion preceding the departure of the Athenian expedition to Sicily. After all the ships had been manned and everything for the journey had been put on board, a silence was proclaimed by the sounding of a trumpet. Then followed the service of prayer customarily held before ships put out to sea. The ceremony was performed in unison, the sailors on each ship participating in the rites. All were prepared for the moment with the proper bowls of wine, and both the seamen and the officers together made their oblations by pouring the wine from gold and silver goblets into the sea. Not only those in the ships but the assembled multitude on the shore, whether they were citizens or any other persons in sympathy with the enterprise, joined in the prayer. The ceremony closed with the singing of a hymn, after which the ships weighed anchor and put out to sea.[10]

Often even the individual made his prayers conform to some standard ritual. It was greatly to his advantage to be able to address a deity by the correct title. If in doubt about the proper terminology, one might pray to Zeus and add, "Whoever he be, if it please him to be named thus, by that title I address him." It was fitting also that special preparation of one's person should be made before approaching the gods in prayer. He who offered his morning libation without having first washed his hands was not to expect that any heed would be paid to his petition. If the prayer was made at the sanctuary, it was to follow the offering of sacrifice and the pouring of libations. While it was usually uttered in the form of petition, it might also be a thanksgiving. Some prayers were long and others brief. The emperor Marcus Aurelius, who was far more Greek than Roman in his personal piety, thought the Athenians had formulated an ideal prayer in the simple petition, "Rain, rain, O beloved Zeus, down upon the fields of the Athenians and upon the plains."[11]

Sometimes no slight fervor manifested itself in connection with prayer, apparently on the assumption that, as the petition became more eloquent, the attention of the deity would be most surely attracted. Pagans, as did Christians, "lifted up their voice" to the god, and, the more urgent the need, the greater was the vehemence of expression. Other petitions were offered in silence, or in low whispers, it being taken for granted that the gods were able to hear even the unexpressed wish of the

[10] Thucydides *History* vi. 32.

[11] Aeschylus *Agamemnon* 165; Hesiod *Works and Days* 724 ff.; Marcus Aurelius *Meditations* v. 7.

suppliant. Many a sensitive soul appreciated the importance of genuineness and sincerity as prime essentials for a successful supplication. Some persons attached a magical significance to the act of prayer, supposing that the use of a proper formula compelled the gods to grant the petition; but there were many others who said that the gods could be neither bribed nor coerced. Correctness of ritual was of some importance, but purity of life and good character on the part of the suppliant was of greater worth. The man who lived piously might reasonably expect a reward for his virtue, while wicked persons ought not to hope for a favorable response. It was the petition of the righteous man that availed most.

The Romans, too, placed much store by prayer. It was commonly believed that not only the safety of the public but also the welfare of the individual depended upon fidelity in supplication to the gods. Great stress was laid on proper form. In the early days when the Latin peoples had been largely concerned with the business of agriculture, all the risks of farm life were safeguarded by definitely formulated prayers repeated on stated occasions. When the Roman people became city dwellers and empire-builders, they still regarded prayer essential for success in their new enterprises. In the course of time they learned more and more to pray in the freer Greek manner, yet they never completely lost the reverence for prescribed formalities that had been so assiduously cultivated by their ancestors.

The practice of prayer among the Romans was especially conspicuous in connection with the affairs of state. Formal prayers were said on many public occasions. In times of war the resort to prayer was particularly urgent, and the rite was performed with great solemnity. In the struggle with the Sabines, Romulus was said to have converted imminent defeat into a glorious victory by a pious appeal to Jupiter. The deity was reminded that the foundations of the city on the Palatine Hill had been laid in accordance with divine instruction. If now he would come once more to the aid of his chosen people, Romulus vowed he would build him a temple as a monument witnessing to posterity that Jupiter had been savior of the Romans. Thus impending disaster had been turned into brilliant victory through the aid of heaven. Similarly, a treaty was sealed in the name of Jupiter, who was invoked to strike down the Roman people, even as the sacrificial swine was slaughtered, if they should ever prove false to their pledge.

In times of peace the prayer life of the Roman people was no less serious and exacting. Before addressing a public assembly, the magistrates were accustomed to pronounce a solemn form of petition. In order that legality might be insured for all that was said, strict attention was given to the maintenance of verbal accuracy. Proper formulas for use on various occasions were collected and preserved in the books of the priests. The ceremonies were very carefully guarded lest a single word should be omitted or pronounced out of its place. In the course of time the prescribed formulas might become unintelligible even to the priest himself, yet they were carefully preserved. They constituted a sacred ritual that no one dared venture to alter.[12]

When mistakes were made in the ritual of prayer, serious consequences were likely to follow. Even the sophisticated

---

[12] Livy *History* xxxix. 15; Pliny *Natural History* xxviii. 2; Aulus Gellius *Attic Nights* xiii. 22; Quintilian *Institutes* i. 6. 40.

Pliny the Elder imagined that violation of correct procedure in the past had been attended by terrifying results. Sometimes the gods indicated their displeasure through strange phenomena manifest in connection with the sacrificial animal. On certain occasions the lobe of the liver or the heart had disappeared, or had been doubled, while the victim stood before the altar. Such strange occurrences were thought to invalidate the petition, rendering it utterly ineffective in its appeal to the deities. The only remedy was to repeat the rites correctly. Also there were instances of neglect on the part of an officiating servant who failed to observe the prayers at the proper time. The omission was so serious that the Senate asked advice of the college of pontiffs, who decreed that the whole festival had been invalidated and would need to be repeated. Once the sacrifice had to be offered thirty times in succession because of some neglect or mistake or accident that had repeatedly occurred in connection with the service.[13] Christians ultimately learned from their Roman predecessors to respect the sanctity of an established ritual.

It was in agreement with ancient Roman tradition that prayer should occupy a conspicuous place in the religion of imperial times. The Augustan celebration of the *saeculares* in the year 17 B.C. is instructive in this connection. Although the sacrifice was performed according to the "Greek rite," it was still the old Roman formality that marked the words of Augustus' prayer to the Fates, whom he entreated to increase the dominion and dignity of the Roman people both at home and abroad.[14]

[13] Pliny *Natural History* xxviii. 2. 11; Plutarch *Coriolanus* xxv. 2.

[14] *Corpus inscriptionum Latinarum*, VI, 32323 (p. 3241).

While formal Roman prayer continued to be carefully cultivated and guarded by the proper authorities, there was
among the people at large an increasing liberty of phrase and
variety of content in the prayers of later times. A change had
come about through contact with the East, as Greek influence
entered this area of interest and more individualistic types of
religion from Asia and Egypt made their contributions to the
life of the Roman Empire. Already in the first century B.C.,
Cicero, following the example of Socrates and Plato, had
made sincerity more important than ritual formality. The
gods were to be approached with purity of soul. Not that the
requirement of ritual correctness was to be ignored, but the
weightier matter of heart righteousness was of primary importance. Pollutions of the body could be removed by a few
ablutions or other cleansing ceremonies of brief duration, but
stains on the soul could not be washed out even by long-
continued rites and by all the rivers in the world. And in
Cicero's own most brilliant example of a literary Roman
prayer, with which he closed his prosecution of Verres, he
implored the gods to influence the judges in pronouncing
condemnation upon the criminal for wickedness, audacity,
perfidy, lust, avarice, and cruelty.

Critics of traditional practices in prayer among the Romans
were numerous in imperial times. Some persons advised
leaving the deities alone to determine for themselves what
was expedient for mankind in general and what specific favor
was appropriate to each individual. Since man was dearer to
the gods than to himself, it would be good taste on the part
of a suppliant to pray for a bold and free spirit and freedom
from dread of death, leaving it to the deities to grant him what

they might think best in other respects. Particularly it should be remembered that the only path to peace lay in the cultivation of virtue; it could not be secured by beseeching the gods for special favors. Juvenal deplored the fact, as he stated it in satire, that the most common prayers heard in the temples were petitions to the gods for the increase of man's wealth.

In the experience of many persons in the imperial age, prayer took on a more spiritual significance. A man of Seneca's temper was confident that prayers could not alter the will and purpose of an all-wise god, yet the sincere suppliant was assured of receiving blessings that otherwise would have been withheld. But the rewards were spiritual rather than material. They were an experience of the soul, such as a heightening of its appreciation of divine wisdom, a more exalted adoration of the deity, and a nearer approach to godlikeness on the part of the worshiper. Seneca read with approval in Athenodorus, the famous Stoic philosopher of Tarsus, that one should suppress unworthy desires by making only such petitions to the deity as one would be willing to offer in public. To which Seneca adds: "So live with men as if god saw, and so speak with god as if men heard." God is not so far away that men must raise their hands toward heaven and shout their requests into the ears of an image. Rather, "he is near you, he is with you, he is in you."[15]

III

The ancients trusted not alone in the efficacy of their prayers to secure the favor of heaven. Many other instruments were employed to effect and maintain safe and profitable

[15] Seneca *Natural Questions* ii. 36–37; *Epistles* i. 10. 5; iv. 12 (41). 1.

relations with the deities. Man sought to honor them by consecrating to them artistic and aesthetic accomplishments in music, architecture, sculpture, and painting. Also, he generously devoted to them a large proportion of such wealth as he possessed. Temples were reared in great abundance, and many of these structures were magnificently adorned and richly endowed. Sacrifices and votive offerings were almost innumerable, and properly equipped priests were maintained at all the sanctuaries. Many sacred days were set aside during the year for public worship, and private rites were always in order.

Apparently from a very early date the Greeks had been accustomed to employ musical devices in their efforts to win the favor of the gods. Homer was authority for the belief that one of the chief and most pious duties belonging to mankind was to hymn the praises of the gods in return for the blessings of speech which had been conferred by heaven upon mankind. Music was especially prominent in the rites of Apollo. After describing the celebration of a feast which began with prayer and closed with a solemn drink-offering to the god, Homer adds: "So all day long they worshiped the god with music, singing the beautiful paean, the sons of the Achaians making music to the far-darter; and his heart was glad to hear."[16] There was something about music that gave to the worshiper himself a sense of nearer proximity to the divine, and, when accompanied by the playing of instruments and dancing, the consequent pleasurable excitation seemed to involve a distinct heightening of religious experience. While

---

[16] *Iliad* i. 470 ff.; cf. Plutarch *Music* ii; Strabo *Geography* x. 3. 9.

moralists might say that men resembled the gods chiefly in doing good, others who were more appreciative of the emotional side of life claimed that man was most godlike when he was happy and that the highest happiness consisted in rejoicing in festivals and in music.

According to Plato, Greek music had originally been divided into certain kinds sharply distinguished from one another. One type had consisted in prayers, called hymns, offered to the gods. In contrast with these more joyous expressions of feeling, there was another type called lamentations, which apparently were connected with the rites of infernal deities whose death was loudly mourned by the devotees. A third type was the paean, the choral song or hymn in honor of Apollo's victory over the Python, and sung in the celebration of the Pythian games. The fourth class was called the dithyramb, of which Plato thinks the subject was the birth of Dionysus.

Music was employed in the worship of various gods. Provision was made in the budget of a cult for the support of temple choirs, which was as truly a religious duty as that of providing for the sacrifice. Pantomime and dancing frequently accompanied the processional hymns sung on the way to the temples. It is not improbable that each temple had its hymnbook containing not only words but also definite melodies. In the Apollo cult the hymns were sung to the accompaniment of the harp, while in the rites of Dionysus the flute was used. Other cults combined the use of different instruments, with results not always pleasing to the cultivated ear but quite inspiring for the masses who participated in the rites. Plato said he could not tolerate the jazz of his day, yet he had a very high appreciation of music in the service of religion.

While the Romans were less inclined than were the Greeks to lend themselves to emotional display in religious ceremonies, they did employ at a very early date hymns as a means of communicating with the gods. There were ancient hymns of Mars, no longer intelligible even to the priests in the Augustan age. Also one hears of the hymn and dance in the ceremonies of the ancient priestly guild of the Arval Brothers. But in order to experience to the full the stimulating effect of music, accompanied by pantomime and dance and other forms of emotional agitation, the Roman people had to resort to one of the Greek or oriental cults. Many Romans participated in the wild orgies of Bacchus, the noisy processions of Cybele, and the moving rites of Isis. In such associations they could enjoy the sense of effective approach to the gods that resulted from the clanging of symbols, the shaking of the sistra, the fingering of the harp, or the blowing of the flute.

The gods were brought still nearer to man by housing them on earth among the humbler dwellings of mortals. Like the ancient Hebrews who built a house for their God, lavishing upon it everything that was most precious in their own society, the Gentiles also reared temples to their various gods. These structures were adorned with man's most beautiful handiwork and enriched with his most precious possessions. If supernatural power were to be made fully available for a seeking humanity, it was highly desirable that the deities should be given permanent and appropriate dwelling places where they might be visited by their devotees. But the sanctity of the deities would not permit of too great familiarity. The most suitable ground for temples and altars was thought to be a conspicuous spot somewhat removed from the everyday activities of men in order that one might not enter the sanctuaries with the stain of secular life too fresh upon one's person. Yet these buildings ought to be open to the view of every man so that, when praying, he could turn his face templeward. Leaving the crowded areas where one had engaged in the commonplace activities of daily living, one performed on the way to the temples such rites of purification as were necessary for proper access to the divine presence.

The Greek and the Roman temples were the most magnificent architectural structures produced in the ancient world. It was fitting that the abodes of the deities should be the largest, the most splendidly adorned, and the most heavily endowed public buildings in the community. Christian preachers found a host of gentile gods already magnificently housed and readily accessible through participation in the elaborate ceremonies connected with the temple. To the average citizen of Ephesus who happened to be at all aware of the presence of Paul and his little group of followers meeting in the room they rented in the school of Tyrannus, the new religious movement must have seemed pathetically insignificant in comparison with the worship of the great Artemis. Her magnificent cathedral towered above the other structures in the city, its foundations covering some two acres of ground. It is little wonder that the Ephesian populace should have been ready to shout themselves hoarse in proclaiming "great is Artemis of the Ephesians" (Acts 19:28). Christians had yet to learn from their gentile rivals the skill needed to rear magnificent buildings to house the activities of their cult.

In the case of the traditional gods of Greece and Rome the temples were built and their support was provided by the community or the state, whose business it was to cultivate supernatural resources for insuring the welfare of society. The choicest portions of land were set aside for this purpose, while funds were generously appropriated for the building of the structure, the financing of festivals, the support of the priesthood, the purchase of victims for the sacrifices, the maintenance of the temple choirs, and all other forms of activity thought to be in accord with the wishes of the deity.

The presence of the deity was made more real by an image conspicuously displayed before the eyes of all who ascended the temple steps to look through the open door. The worshipers saw their god in visible form, and in the decorations of the building, in its sculpture and its paintings, they read the story of the god's doings and saw many an evidence of his interest in their welfare. In these portrayals by their best artists the people were provided with pictorial exhibitions of the theology of the rites which in this form had greater reality and meaning for the average person than would ever have been possible had his religious traditions been presented in books systematically formulating the dogma of the cult. Men knew that the deities were kind and capable because the assurance of this fact was placarded before their eyes. Similarly, Paul endeavored to appeal to eye as well as ear by exhibiting in word-pictures to his Galatian and Corinthian congregations the image of Jesus Christ and him crucified (Gal. 3:1; I Cor. 2:2).

Sometimes the temples were richly endowed, thus making the prosperity of the deity surpass that of the ordinary worshiper. Wealthy individuals built temples at their own expense and subsidized their upkeep by grants of land or other emoluments. Some people willed their property to the temple or even handed it over before death in consideration of a stipend for life. Often one temple owned property in several places. There are many inscriptions that list such holdings and specify their income. Certain bodies of water were consecrated to a god, and the fish might not be caught, or else they were the property of the priests. Other sacred property consisted of woodlands, of pastures rented to shepherds, of fields cultivated by farmers, of gardens and houses and factories. The propriety of conceding to the deity title to a large share of land or business or other sources of wealth was a well-established idea in the gentile world long before the Christian notion of church property and papal states arose.

The offering of sacrifice was a fundamental necessity in any attempt to win and maintain the divine favor. Of the Gentiles it might truly be said that there was no salvation without the shedding of blood. Purification, expiation, and atonement conditioned all efforts to live on favorable terms with the gods. The correct procedure in the operation of these sacred rites was insured through the maintenance of a properly instructed priesthood. While the customary sacrifices seem to have been thought sufficient under ordinary circumstances to maintain the divine favor, there might be critical moments demanding unusual offerings. The greatest gift that could be presented to the deity to expiate man's sin and avert the wrath of heaven was the life of a human being. A few conspicuous examples of human sacrifice were known to Roman tradition, and the fact that it was no longer tolerated in imperial times only added to the prestige of the traditional stories from ancient times.

One story was especially noteworthy. When three vestal virgins had been found guilty of violating their vow of chastity, the crime seemed so heinous that the whole people needed purification. Nothing short of human sacrifice would, it was felt, avert impending calamity. The Sibylline Books were consulted and yielded instructions that two men and two women, two of them Greeks and two Gauls, should be buried alive in the Forum. Plutarch, accepting this tradition as fact, offered an interesting explanation of the occurrence. He knew that human sacrifice to the gods had long before become illegal among the Romans. How, then, could they violate their own laws? Plutarch reasoned that the demand for human victims had been made by demons, to whom the sacrifice was rendered. It had been performed not as a gift to the great Roman deities but "in order to appease some alien and foreign demons." In later days there were Christians who could talk in a similar way about the sacrificial death of Jesus as a price paid to the devil.[17]

The ancient man never forgot that gods and mortals belonged, respectively, in the realms of the holy and the profane. The temples were sacred places never to be defiled with impunity. The worshiper might not approach them until he had purified himself in both body and soul. There was in every temple of Apollo a holy water with which the devotee might purge himself before entering the sanctuary. At other times he went down to the sea to perform his cleansing rites. The pious

---

[17] Plutarch *Roman Questions* lxxxiii; cf. *Cessation of Oracles* xvi.

man gave himself very diligently to such ablutions, even though a Diogenes might cynically inform him that he could as successfully wash away blunders in his grammar as purify his soul by ceremonial means.[18]

When Christian missionaries first set out upon the task of convincing Gentiles that the only way of access to the true God was through faith in the hero Jesus, the representatives of the new cause were pitifully lacking in anything like an elaborately organized and officered institution. The spontaneous outburst in a prayer, the emotional expression of a prophecy or a psalm, a baptismal rite performed without reference to any officiating minister or priest, the similarly unconventional observance of a memorial meal celebrating the death of their hero, and their heritage of scriptural reading and teaching taken over from Judaism were all that Christians had to offer in the way of institutional machinery for a correct and effective approach to the supernatural powers. But in time they learned how to construct and employ a much more complicated technique modeled after the pattern already in use among their gentile contemporaries.

Ultimately, Christians elaborated and formalized their prayers; they more adequately officered their institution; they set apart priests, clothing them in distinctive garments and assigning them definite functions; they built structures for housing the deity, adorning them with the full heritage of gentile art and displaying upon their walls the legends and history of the new cult; and they filled their churches with statues of their savior and their saints. They set aside holy days

[18] Diogenes Laertius vi. 2. 42; Ovid *Fasti* ii. 38 ff.

and celebrated festivals in elaborate fashion. By the end of the second century a Christian could boast that the disciples of Christ spent more time in their one great celebration of fifty days between Easter and Pentecost than was consumed by all the heathen festivals during the whole year. Thus Christianity triumphed not by abolishing the yearning of the heathen for access to the supernatural but by intensifying and heightening the customary techniques for attaining this goal.

CHAPTER VI

SUPERNATURAL PROTECTION FOR SOCIETY

REVERENCE paid to the deities was believed to have its abundant rewards. Everything was a concern of the gods. No one could evade their all-seeing gaze and no area of experience lay beyond the range of their operations. Only the Epicurean felt himself immune from their intervention for good or for evil; the rest of humanity trembled in fear or rejoiced in confidence under the ever present shadow of the divinities. If not with the same degree of assurance, at least with a similar feeling of inevitability, many a Gentile could have exclaimed with the Hebrew psalmist that it was impossible to escape from deity even though one might mount to the dome of the heavens, descend to the darkest cavern of the lower regions, or take flight on the wings of the morning to the farthest bounds of the ocean.

Inescapable gods constituted both a menace and a blessing. The ancient man had created the deities out of the raw material of his experience, which had taught him that his environing world could be both hostile and kindly by turns. One who had profited by the relatively well-ordered conditions of the Roman Empire was inclined to believe that, on the whole, the supernatural powers were well disposed, at least toward all individuals of good standing in society. Prosperity spelled divine protection, and its evidences seemed abundantly dis-

121

played under the efficient rule of Augustus. A new sense of safety was shared generally by the subjects of Rome from the Pillars of Hercules to the borders of Mesopotamia.

I

At the beginning of the Christian Era the organized Roman state was a truly marvelous institution. People of that day were sure that its like had never before been known. Its antiquity, its well-nigh boundless domains, and the efficiency of its governmental machinery seemed to attest its supernatural excellence.

As early as the second century B.C., after Rome had destroyed Carthage and conquered Greece, there were studious observers of the political situation who, although not themselves Romans, recognized the superior greatness of the new victor in comparison with all previously known world powers. Even the vast empire of Alexander had been narrow in range and of brief duration in contrast with the expanding kingdom of the Romans. A century before the establishment of the Empire under Augustus, the Greek historian Polybius believed that already in his day the Roman arms had conquered practically the whole inhabited world and instituted a government destined to remain unrivaled throughout all future time. It quite surpassed any similar foundation known to the past. In the next century when the Roman domains had been further extended and the republican form of government had given place to the Augustan regime, admiration for imperialism found frequent expression. Above all, it was thought to be the unique mission of Rome to provide society throughout the whole Mediterranean world with protection for life and property and to supply mankind with an unfailing and effective political administration. While the Romans might not be destined to excel other peoples like the Greeks in sculpture and rhetoric and philosophy, it was still their duty to give the world the most enduring and beneficent political order that had ever been experienced by man.[1]

Belief in the eternity of the Roman state was frequently reiterated. As a foundation of the gods it was to endure forever. Popular tradition affirmed that the temple of Vesta housed an image that had fallen from heaven and that, if it was faithfully guarded, the Roman commonwealth would endure throughout all future time. Romans spoke of the "Eternal City" which had been founded by Romulus and of the "eternal fires" kept constantly burning in the vestal shrine as the pledge of perpetual dominion. When in consequence of an attendant's neglect the fires had once gone out, they had been miraculously restored by the prayer of the priestess who threw a piece of her linen garment on the extinguished altar where the cloth immediately burst into flame. Rome's title to perpetuity was thought to rest upon a far more stable basis than that of leadership by any general or other high official who might temporarily guide her destiny. It was absurd to imagine that a city built under the auspices and sanctions of the gods and destined for eternity could have her existence conditioned by the frail body of any mortal. She was as enduring as the heavens and as stable as the cosmos.[2]

The chief glory of Rome lay in the protection she furnished

---

[1] Vergil *Aeneid* vi. 845 ff.; Dionysius of Halicarnassus *Roman Antiquities* i. 2–3.

[2] Cicero *Phillippic* xi. 10. 24; Tibullus *Elegy* ii. 5. 13; Horace *Odes* iii. 5. 11; Livy *History* iv. 4. 4; xxvi. 27. 14; xxviii. 28. 11; Dionysius of Halicarnassus *Roman Antiquities* ii. 68.

society. However much the people might be exploited in the interests of the government, its efficiency gave them a quite new sense of national safety. They remembered keenly those previous periods in history when civil wars or an inadequate administration had often resulted in suffering and chaos. They were ready to welcome the dawn of a new day, and they visualized the new order in the imagery of supernaturalism. A militaristic machine created by heaven would bring into being the social stability universally craved by the entire population. Tibullus and Vergil shudderingly recalled the degeneracy of an earlier age when, under the rule of Jupiter, "slaughter and swords were incessant"; and they prophesied the coming of a new day—the return of Saturn's rule—when a new king should appear "under whom first the iron age shall cease and the golden age over all the world arise."

Augustan imperialism was widely accepted as the fulfilment of gentile "messianic" hopes. The world at last was safe because the government of Augustus was firmly and permanently established. The hope of mankind for the future lay in the expected maintenance of this political order throughout all ages to come. Pliny the Elder, notwithstanding his show of opposition to other superstitions, had no difficulty in believing that it was Rome's mission "to unite the scattered empires of the earth, to bestow a polish upon men's manners, to unite the discordant and uncouth dialects of so many different nations by the powerful ties of one common language, to confer the enjoyments of discourse and civilization upon mankind, and to become the mother country of all nations."[3]

Now and then a Stoic, with his characteristic emphasis on

[3] *Natural History* iii. 5. 39; xxvii. 1. 3.

humanitarianism, ventured to criticize popular faith in imperialism's efficacy to redeem society from its ills. Seneca, for example, was particularly severe in his arraignment of the military operations pursued in support of the imperial program. He ridiculed the folly of those human beings who sought to fix tribal boundaries and fought for control of territory. Would ants, he sarcastically asked, if ever they should become endowed with human intelligence, apportion the threshing floor into many provinces? In his opinion, the laudation of Roman imperialism was mainly a cloak to shield pride and avarice. In writing of the winds, he remarked that the deity did not intend them to be used for military advantage by providing means for carrying fleets of armed soldiers to every quarter of the world. Such enterprises were a desecration of the sea and the land, in which men were worse than beasts. The latter fought only in retaliation, or from hunger, but men poured out their own and others' blood simply for greed of gold.[4]

While the Stoic preached the doctrine of human brotherhood and lauded the blessings of peace, he never devised any really effective program for the accomplishment of his ideals. On the other hand, the imperial organization was busy perfecting itself from the very beginning of the Augustan age and proved so successful in maintaining a state of peace and prosperity superior to that which had previously been known to the Mediterranean world that popular faith in the beneficent significance of the Roman political organization became more and more widespread. There was as yet no thought that mankind could realize protection and safety for itself

[4] Seneca *Natural Questions* v. 18. 4 ff.

through the establishment of a strictly democratic form of government. The assurances of successful politics were assumed to come from without; they were not sought in the inherent potentialities of human society. Good government was a gift of the gods.

Both Jews and Christians bore similar testimony to the beneficent regime of Augustus. Although they were unwilling to deify an emperor, they were quite ready to recognize that the new day which he had inaugurated in Roman history was an evidence of heaven's interest in the welfare of mankind. The favor which Augustus had shown to the Jews in respecting their traditional religious customs, and particularly his care to provide a regular sacrifice for himself at the Jewish temple in Jerusalem, seemed to Philo to insure the success and perpetuity of the Roman government. An empire that thus made an appeal to the Hebrew God would endure without end. Augustus had done well to ordain a continual sacrifice of burnt offerings to be observed "forever and ever, every day from his own revenues, as a first fruit of his own to the most high God, which sacrifices are performed to this very day and will be performed forever as a proof and specimen of a truly imperial disposition."

Philo thought it quite fitting that a Roman emperor who displayed such piety toward the God of the Hebrews should be highly praised for the benefits which his rule had bestowed upon mankind. This devout prince was capable of calming storms that had been raging in every quarter of the earth and of healing the social diseases that heretofore had sorely afflicted the residents of the lands about the Mediterranean. Philo believed that at the time of Augustus' rise to power the

world had been in a very bad way. Every territory had been
filled with unexpected miseries, but the new ruler had delivered all men from their distresses. He gave them not only a
temporary release from the bonds of their affliction, but he
completely broke all those fetters by which the entire habit-
able earth had previously been enchained. Having brought all
wars to an end, he had made the whole world one great arena
of peace: "This is he who gave freedom to every city, who set
chaos in order, who civilized and made obedient and harmo-
nious nations which before his time were unsociable, hostile
and brutal."[5]

In the second century, when Christianity began to seek
recognition from the Roman state, Christians praised the feats
of Augustus as readily as did Gentiles and Hellenistic Jews.
But they offered their distinctive interpretation of the basis
upon which emperors had been the recipient of divine favor.
Melito, bishop of Sardis, when addressing Marcus Aurelius,
admitted that Christianity had been originally a barbarian
movement but called attention particularly to the fact that
the new religion had arisen in the time of Augustus and thus
had become for the Empire an especial blessing of auspicious
omen. From that time the power of Rome had grown in
greatness and splendor. Its glory had continued undimmed
throughout two centuries and would endure for all time, if
the government showed itself favorable toward and appreciative of Christianity. This observation seemed especially significant to Melito, who added that "a most convincing proof
that our doctrine flourished for the good of an empire happily
begun is this, namely, that there has no evil happened since

[5] Philo *To Gaius* xxi. 147; xxiii. 157; cf. Josephus *Antiquities* xvi. 38 ff.

Augustus ruled, but on the contrary all things have been blessed and glorious in accordance with the prayers of all."[6]

It early became a commonly accepted belief among Christians that the unification of the Mediterranean lands under the beneficent rule of Augustus had been an event divinely ordered with a view to preparing the world for the reception of Christianity. A politically unified world with a universal language seemed to have been prearranged by God himself in order that this unity among nations under the rule of one prince might make it easier for the apostles of Jesus to make disciples throughout the entire world. Wars between rival political powers had to be stopped by God in order that men might have time to hear the gospel. "How was it possible," says Origen in his reply to Celsus, "for the gospel doctrine of peace, which does not permit men to take vengeance even upon their enemies, to prevail throughout the world unless at the advent of Jesus a milder spirit had been everywhere introduced into the conduct of affairs." Thus for Christians, as for their heathen rivals, the Roman Empire was an establishment of heaven for the benefit of mankind.

II

The Romans did not need to be told by Jews and Christians that heaven had intervened in Roman politics to make possible unaccustomed blessings for humanity. When Philo intimated that the prosperity and peace of the early imperial age had been due to the willingness of Augustus to pay respect to the God of the Hebrews, or when the Christian Melito affirmed that this happy state of affairs had been divinely in-

[6] Eusebius *Church History* iv. 26. 7–8.

stituted to prepare the way for the success of Christianity, these foreign preachers were only repeating in variant form an idea they had already learned from their heathen contemporaries. It was a fundamental belief among the Romans that, not only under the Empire, but throughout the whole course of their history, political success had depended on the favor of the gods. The Roman government was essentially a kingdom of heaven, an establishment of the deities, a successful kingdom of this world because a creation and constant care of the supernatural powers whose help for society was made concretely available by means of political institutions.

It had long been characteristic of ancient society to provide political organizations with religious sanctions. Not infrequently the king included in his responsibilities both sacerdotal and political functions. He was a servant of the deity and a helper of the people in one and the same person. In the case of the Pharaohs, for instance, the prince was so active in the performance of religious rites that one sometimes finds difficulty in distinguishing between the royal and the priestly duties of the ruler. The laws which he promulgated, the wars in which he engaged, and the ceremonies of his court were all fortified by ample divine sanctions. A similar fusion of religion and politics was indicated in the famous legal code issued by the Babylonian Hammurabi as a revelation from the deity. The conquering monarchs of Assyria believed themselves victorious through the favor of their god Ashur. The same reliance on divine protection characterized smaller nations, like the Moabites, who ascribed their victory over the Hebrews to the favor of their local god Chemosh. The Hebrews of Palestine, in turn, were equally confident that a successful political organization for them would be impossible except as they were ruled by a prince whom God himself had anointed to administer their government. An efficient political administration, competent to give society a full measure of protection, was thought possible only in the form of a divinely established institution.

In the matter of supernatural safeguards for society's well-being, the faith of the Greeks did not fall behind that of their Asiatic and Egyptian neighbors. The Greek city-states trusted in patron deities, and heaven was believed to have displayed its keen interest in the establishment of centers of culture through granting immortality and deification to the reputed heroic founders of many different cities. Oracles were consulted, especially at critical moments in the course of history, and individuals who were thought to menace faith in the gods were punished as enemies of the state. It was said that famous lawgivers like Solon and Lycurgus derived their wisdom from Apollo, and there were those who believed that "every law is an invention and gift of the gods." When victorious over the aggressive Persians, the Greeks credited their triumph ultimately to the deities in whom they had placed their trust. While the Greeks were never successful in welding themselves into a united nation, they were nonetheless confident that their separate groups, in organizing their governmental machinery for the protection of life and property, were operating not simply as human institutions but as supernaturally protected societies.[7]

In the later history of the Greeks, Alexander the Great was

----

[7] See Pseudo-Demosthenes *Against Aristogiton* i. 15; Plato *Laws* 699; Herodotus *History* viii. 109.

shown to be a model of piety in his reliance on the gods. At the beginning of his expedition into Asia he had taken elaborate pains to insure divine favor for his gigantic enterprise. Before setting out, he had erected altars to Athena and Hercules. While crossing the Hellespont, he had sacrificed to Poseidon and the other gods of the sea. Again on disembarking in Asia, he reared altars to Zeus, Athena, and Hercules. He went to Ilium, where he performed further religious ceremonies in honor of Trojan Athena, depositing his panoply as a votive offering in the temple in exchange for some consecrated relics of the Trojan War which were carried before him into battle. He was said to have been "strictly observant of his duty to the gods." Later generations who thus idealized the political career of Alexander made his empire essentially a kingdom of heaven.[8]

The successors of Alexander were clothed with a like divine authority. The Ptolemies in Egypt and the Seleucid rulers in Syria seemed in the eyes of their subjects to be manifest embodiments of the deities' favor for the existing governments. When their kingdoms came to an end with the Romans' assumption of responsibility for setting in order political affairs in the East, Roman generals and emperors were readily endowed by their Eastern subjects with divine epithets marking them as ruling by the authority of the gods. But this ideal of a supernaturally ordered state was not unfamiliar to the Roman people even before they had made conquest of the East.

It is very true that the oldest form of Roman religion was not primarily political in its emphasis. In the earlier years of

[8] Arrian *Anabasis* i. 11; vii. 28.

their experience the crucial points at which the Romans had
felt the need of supernatural guardians had been the door at
which an enemy might enter the household, the hearth where
the women cooked the food, the store chamber where supplies
were kept, and the boundary stone of the farm under cultivation. In later years, when the organization of government
became a more crucial problem, the interpreters of Roman
history were able to look back with much satisfaction upon
the primitive period where they found it easy to discover that
all Rome's political antecedents had been fortified by ample
supernatural sanctions.

The pious Roman was as firmly convinced as the devout
Hebrew that the city of his fathers and the state that had
grown up around this center were a divine foundation. Livy,
who was himself somewhat skeptical of popular tradition,
could nevertheless concede that if any people had a right to
make the gods the authors of their government, certainly the
Romans were entitled to that privilege. Romulus had built
Rome under the guidance of the gods whose will had been
communicated to him by vultures. Since these birds were
accustomed to blood and prey, the occurrence was thought to
presage a brilliant career for the new foundation. Romulus
had further insured heaven's favor by giving strict attention
to the most approved religious rites. Romans of the Augustan
age believed that in no other newly built city could one have
found so many priests and ministers of the deities and so much
care for religious procedures as in Rome during this primitive
period of national history.[9]

[9] Livy *History* Preface 7; Dionysius of Halicarnassus *Antiquities* ii. 18. 21;
Florus *History* i. 1.

Of all Rome's ancient worthies, Numa seems to have been thought the supreme model of piety. In his ministrations the greatest assurances of supernatural help had been evident. He, like the Hebrew Saul, was credited with having waited upon the will of heaven before accepting his election to kingship. Not until the augurs had reported unmistakable signs of the divine approval would he accede to the people's request that he become their ruler. Accordingly, he passed his whole reign in peace and demonstrated clearly in his administration of the government that he was unusually favored with wisdom from the gods. Like a veritable Moses to the Romans, he set in order and elaborated the system of religious observances by which his descendants could henceforth shape their conduct in a fashion pleasing to the deities.[10]

The Romans were well aware that their past had not been uniformly prosperous. The career of a state that had begun under the favor of heaven ought, from the ideal point of view, to have been immune from those distresses which had so often overtaken Roman society in the course of centuries of history. At such times had the gods temporarily failed to perform their duty? Manifestly in periods of threatening disaster their favor had been withdrawn, and the Romans, attached as they were to the theory of divine protection for the state, had only one explanation to offer. Disaster had been due to the people's neglect of the deities. Lack of fidelity in the observance of sacred ceremonies was the inevitable forerunner of calamity, while assiduous observance of established rites was a guaranty of prosperity. If Roman society had suffered agonies, it was be-

[10] Dionysius of Halicarnassus *Antiquities* ii. 60 ff.; Livy *History* i. 20; Plutarch *Numa* viii.

cause the government had not always been conducted in accordance with the prescribed rites of ancient religion. A faithful return to traditional customs was the only sure remedy for present ills.[11]

As the death agonies of the Republic proved to be the birth pangs ushering in the new Empire, both the disasters connected with the passing of the old order and the happier state of affairs inaugurated by the new were closely associated with the action of supernatural powers. Many a writer remarked upon the decay of religion in the later years of the Republic and blamed it on the contact with Greece following the destruction of Carthage. Under the influence of Greek skeptical philosophy, some men had boldly denied the existence of the gods or had affirmed that they took no part in the conduct of human affairs. The traditionalists were scandalized by this skepticism. Varro expressed alarm lest the Roman gods should perish from sheer neglect by the people, and Cicero warned his contemporaries that to cast off piety toward the deities would bring chaos to society. While Varro and Cicero took a pragmatic view of the value of religion to the Roman state, others saw in the disasters of civil war that attended the fall of the Republic the working of supernatural agencies punishing the Romans for their laxity in religion. Indifference toward religion had been a disaster to the state.

That the fall of the Republic was really according to the will of heaven was most clearly discerned after the event and by those who were most closely connected with the new regime. It is easy to accuse Augustus of insincerity in his religious

---

[11] Cicero *Nature of the Gods* ii. 3; Livy *History* xxi. 62.

reforms, but undoubtedly he entertained the traditional Roman belief in a god-protected state. Not only does the literature produced under his patronage glow with satisfaction and confidence born of an assurance that the political order is a superhuman creation, but the emperor himself expended a vast amount of energy and capital upon the restoration of priesthoods and temples and the machinery for doing business with the supernatural powers. Assuredly he did not wish to be classed among those perfidious persons of the past who were blamed for having brought misfortune on the Romans through neglect of religion.

Above all others, Vergil was the prophet of the new day. In his oft-quoted fourth *Eclogue* he boldly forecast the early end of the times of agony and the rise of a new political order to exhibit more perfectly the kindly will of heaven. Men would then be liberated from their age-old fears, while only a few stains of the old-time sin would survive. Under the rule of a new heaven-sent prince the earth would bring forth her fruits spontaneously, the warring elements in nature would be transformed into agencies of peace, the lion would no longer prey upon the ox, the serpent and the poisonous herbs would be exterminated, and foreign spice plants would grow uncultivated in every field. The ripening grain would no more be smitten by blight, grapes would grow in abundance on the bramble, and the sturdy oak would drip honey.

Vergil was more fortunate than most prophets in living to see the day when he could believe that his predictions had come true. With the institution of the regime of Augustus the care of the gods for Roman politics seemed amply demonstrated. Now the poet could declare with confidence that in

the new Empire one saw the fulfilment of an ancient promise
that Ilia should bear to the loins of Mars twin children from
whom should arise a state whose fortunes would know no
bounds and whose power would never wane.[12] It was this
state of mind that made possible among the Romans the
growing popularity of that astonishing phenomenon known
as emperor-worship. While the deification of Eastern princes
supplied ample precedents for the practice, it owed its vitality
among the Romans chiefly to their custom of seeking political
prosperity through an appeal to supernatural powers.

Not only the people who were governed but the officials
themselves commonly assumed an inseparable connection
between religion and politics. Culturally, the rulers were often
one with the masses in their devotion to superstitious beliefs.
They were quite as anxious as were their subjects to see to it
that in the discharge of the duties of their office the favor of
heaven was insured and the anger of the gods averted. One
must not assume that the average Roman ruler thought the
religious ceremonies connected with his administration to be a
mere formality devoid of ultimate significance except as
they produced a desirable impression on his subjects. There
were officials who were at heart Epicurean skeptics and looked
on the idea of a supernatural guidance for political affairs as
mere sham; but, in the main, people in authority in the state
shared fully in the thinking characteristic of that day and
acted genuinely on the conviction that the government they
represented was a creation and a care of the gods, who by
this means were insuring to society a truly divine protection.

[12] *Aeneid* i. 172 ff.

III

For Christians also religion was the only sure foundation on which to erect a permanently ideal state. But the earliest Christians had not imagined that a genuine Kingdom of God was to be established after the model of Roman imperialism. The ancestry of their imagery was Jewish rather than Roman. The kingdoms of this world were all destined to pass away on the day of Christ's return from heaven with his conquering angelic host to overthrow all earthly rulers and establish a heavenly kingdom. In the meantime it was the distinctive task of the disciples of Jesus to gather together a group of the faithful prepared for citizenship in the new regime. They were not to make friends with earthly princes or to seek prestige and office in the existing political institutions. Their supreme duty was to preach the gospel of their risen and returning Christ and gather a company of believers prepared to receive "the Son of Man when he cometh in the glory of his Father, with the holy angels" (Mark 8:38).

In the meantime Christians patiently submitted to the existing forms of government, since God permitted them to exercise a temporary authority. It was not the task of Christians either to overthrow these earthly institutions or to transform them into a more godly type of administration. The existing laws were to be obeyed, taxes were to be paid, and Christians were to exercise great care in avoiding any form of conduct that might be interpreted as resistance to these temporary authorities. Disobedience on the part of Christians was justified only when earthly rulers made such demands on them as required disloyalty to their own king, the Lord Jesus

Christ, to whom they owed supreme allegiance, but whose kingdom was not of this world.

With the passing of the years and the further postponement of Jesus' return, the problem of the relation between church and state became a more crucial one for the growing Christian movement. The authorities showed increasingly a disposition to take sides with those who resisted the Christian preachers and, in the course of time, became active persecutors of the new religion. The growing popularity of emperor-worship in the eastern Mediterranean lands, where Christianity was spreading, created further embarrassment. While a Christian was willing to pay his taxes to secular authorities and to obey all other laws of the heathen state, he could not submit to the popular demand to render divine honors to the emperor. In the presence of the many gods and lords to whom the Gentiles yielded their allegiance, the Christian stoutly affirmed that his supreme loyalty was to Christ alone. In the last analysis the kingdoms of this world belonged to Satan and were due for ultimate destruction by Christ.

The Christian program for the ultimate safety of society, by means of a catastrophic destruction of all evil powers and the establishment of a new kingdom through the descent of Jesus from heaven, ultimately underwent a very radical revision. In the course of a few centuries a complete union between Christianity and the Roman state was effected. It is an astonishing phenomenon to witness the acceptance of this new religion by a government bound up with the heritages and customs of a thousand years of heathenism. But it is no less astonishing that a religious movement which began with the conviction that "all the kingdoms of the world and the glory of them" were proper possessions of Satan should ultimately hail with approval so close a union with Roman imperialism as to make it possible for Christianity to become the divine sponsor of the Roman state. But perhaps this evolution of history will seem less surprising if one fully appreciates at the outset that both Christianity and Roman imperialism were in fundamental agreement at one important point. They both held to the belief that, whatever form of political regime might be instituted for the protection of society, it rested ultimately on a supernatural foundation.

At the outset it was the Roman belief in a divinely authorized state that inspired Rome's policy of hostility to the Christian movement. The characteristic charge brought against Christians was, in effect, that they were enemies of society. They held secret meetings, they indulged in private religious rites, and they refused to participate in local traditional religious activities. When put to the test, they would not acknowledge the lordship of Caesar. They declared that the traditional gods of the state were not gods but merely demons. It is easy to perceive how Christians would incur the hostility of the authorities who sought to please the gods in order to preserve the welfare of the state.

It was entirely natural that the Roman authorities should seek to correct what to them was the atheism of the Christians. The Romans never concerned themselves with specific items of Christian teaching to prove their doctrines false, but it was their intolerable practice that caused offense. Nor was there any serious complaint on the ground that Christianity was another foreign cult. Foreign religions were facts with which Roman society had now become thoroughly familiar and generally tolerant. What made the Christians especially conspicuous was their unwillingness to worship the traditional gods and to confess the lordship of the ruling emperor. This exclusiveness distinguished the Christians from the adherents of other cults who were unmolested by the authorities. The Christians were called atheists not because it was thought that they refused to believe in any god but because they refused to worship the official deities of the state. This stand seemed to threaten the very foundations of political safety as interpreted by the characteristic psychology of the imperial age.

Following the death of Marcus Aurelius in the year 180, the affairs of the Roman government became constantly more precarious. The incursions of the barbarians multiplied, and the breakdown of the social order was increasingly evident. As these distresses mounted, the need for restoring the favor of the gods was felt to be more imperative. It was the best emperors who faced the situation most seriously, and it was also these same rulers who were the most severe persecutors of Christians. This was an entirely proper situation according to the standards of contemporary Roman thinking. Any emperor who sought seriously to stay the forces of disintegration in Roman society undertook to restore the rites of religion as the only sure corrective for the evils of the day. The more numerous Christians became, the greater was the danger to the state from their refusal to revere those supernatural sources of help which were assumed to be the only adequate guarantors of safety for the state.

In their efforts to alleviate the distresses of the times, the more capable rulers sought not only to restore the worship of the traditional gods but to supplement their apparently waning power by the introduction of new divinities who could be associated with those of tradition. Inevitably they turned to the East for these new increments of supernatural power. In the second and third Christian centuries gods from the Orient were serving far more conspicuously the needs of the Roman government than were the native deities of Italy. In the reforms of Diocletian, for example, which were the most thoroughgoing that had been instituted since the time of Augustus, it was really the invincible sun-god of Syria to whom the Romans attached themselves in the hope of insuring restoration and permanence to their tottering empire. After the retirement of Diocletian, when he and his former colleagues met for a conference at Carnuntum to devise plans for averting the growing menace of political disintegration, their first act was to restore in that city one of the temples of this oriental deity. By paying him this new attention, they evidently thought they would secure a new increment of divine help for healing the ills of the distressed social order.

Just as Diocletian had been one of the most industrious emperors in his efforts to rehabilitate the state, so he had also been one of the severest persecutors of Christianity. His procedure was thoroughly consistent with traditional Roman thinking. Since Christians refused to worship the divine protectors of the state, they incurred the displeasure of its gods and thus were a menace to its welfare. By refusing them the privilege of worshiping their non-Roman deity, it was hoped that they would return in loyalty to the gods of the state, whose favor for the government would thus be enhanced. But the persecution of Diocletian was soon discovered to be a failure, for the Christians, when required to worship the gods of the

state, either obeyed only halfheartedly or else positively refused to yield to the imperial demands. Since the Christians
were no longer allowed to pray to their own God and refused
to pray to any other, the number of channels by which divine
power might be drawn down from heaven into the service
of the government was actually being reduced. Already the
Christians were offering the help of their deity in the affairs
of the state for whose health they continually prayed, and
presently the persecutors decided that it might be better to
accept this assistance, small though it might be, than to deny a
considerable element of the population any rites of worship.

It dawned upon the emperor Galerius that it would be wise
to reverse the older policy in dealing with Christians. On per-
ceiving that great numbers of Christians, when prevented
from worshiping their distinctive God, did not worship the
gods of the state, he issued an edict of toleration permitting
Christians to resume their assemblies and pray for the welfare
of the commonwealth. The charge sometimes laid at the door
of Galerius by Christian historians that he acted insincerely or
the assertion that he mollified his earlier attitude because he
felt death to be near at hand are explanations for which our
sources of information offer no real justification. Galerius was
to the very end a true exponent of the traditional religious
policy of Roman imperialism; he sought to secure every possible measure of supernatural aid for the help of the government.

Constantine's attitude toward Christianity, when he and his
colleague Licinius granted toleration two years later, was
essentially that of Galerius. Constantine was interested in
religion because it supported the state through appeal to

supernatural power. He said explicitly that he granted to
Christians, as well as to all others, full permission to follow
whatever worship they might choose in order that whatever
divinity there is in heaven might be favorably disposed toward
the Roman government and its rulers.

When the emperors made overtures, they found the Christians ready to respond. Even as early as the second century
some leaders in the church had discovered that the real basis
of imperial hostility was a fear that Christians were dangerous
to the state because their "atheism" was supposed to threaten
its religious foundations. On learning this, Christians gradually changed their original attitude of indifference or hostility to politics and affirmed vigorously that they were ready
to pray for emperors and to assert that the adherents of the
new religion constituted the most valuable element in imperial
society because they themselves were in league with the God
of gods, the supreme creator and master of the universe. On
one point only were Christians unyielding. They refused to
worship any deities except those of their own cult, their Lord
Jesus Christ and the God whom they had taken over from
their Hebrew predecessors. But they unblushingly declared
themselves to be the most honest people in the state, the most
ready to pay taxes, and the most zealous and effective in their
prayers on behalf of the commonwealth.

Ultimately, belief in the eternity and divine foundation of
the Roman state became as essential for the Christian theologians as it had formerly been for the old Roman politicians.
The marriage between the Christian religion and Roman
politics became a perfectly legitimate and divinely authenti-
cated union. This outcome was really a much more radical

change in the Christian attitude, as compared with earlier views, than was the change which the emperors underwent when they admitted Christianity among the recognized religions of the state, or even when they made it the only legal religion. When at last Theodosius determined to risk all in the keeping of the Christian's God, he was perpetuating identically the same state of mind that had prompted Augustus to seek out for his kingdom those supernatural sponsors which were believed in his day to be the only adequate sources of protection for a successful government. In adopting Christianity, Roman emperors departed less radically from the psychology of their predecessors than did Christians in becoming Roman imperialists.

CHAPTER VII

DIVINE HELP FOR THE INDIVIDUAL

GODS who protected the Roman state were necessarily more concerned with the welfare of society in general than with the specific needs of the individual. One could not easily imagine that deities intrusted with the guardianship of the Empire's broad domains would have either time or inclination to devote themselves with desired specialization to the needs of every member of its large and varied population. The gods of the state were busy with many great duties. The operations of the government under their care were extensive and complex. Protection had to be insured for armies on far-flung borders, for crops in widely separated areas, for commerce over a broad expanse of sea, and for the prosperity of many large cities. Divinities responsible for world affairs on so vast a scale could hardly be expected to concern themselves with the health of a sick slave in an Egyptian village or with the fate of a wounded gladiator dying in a Roman arena.

It is not surprising that fatalism cast its sinister shadow over a large part of the Roman world. It was only natural that the individual should have felt himself as helpless in his relations with supernatural powers, imperialized after the model of the Roman state, as he was helpless to procure personal favors from the mighty world-ruling prince residing in the imperial palace. But not all men were ready to surrender their faith in the possibility of divine assistance for even the humblest member of society. If the official gods of the state were no longer capable of serving the common man, then new deities had to be found for that purpose. As a matter of fact, there never was a period in the history of ancient peoples when gods who served individuals were more diligently sought, or were thought to be more active, than in the imperial age. Supernatural help was made abundantly available for every man irrespective of his status in society, notwithstanding the tremendously complicated and varied necessities which the complex conditions of the day imposed on the life of mankind in the Roman world .

I

In early stages of civilization, when groups were small and the range of their activities was confined within narrow limits, the well-being of every person seemed adequately safeguarded through membership in a local community. The deities who presided over a specific territory were protectors of every phase of life in that particular region. They insured the fertility of the soil, the perpetuity of the race, the preservation of health, and the success of all activities undertaken by the group, or by individuals in the group, to maintain the prosperity and perpetuity of their cultural status. One needed no personal access to the deity, because the life of the individual was thoroughly integrated in the life of the community.

In the Roman Empire a very different situation prevailed. The world of both gods and men had become far too cosmopolitan to permit the average person to imagine that all his interests were sufficiently protected simply by allegiance to the gods of his fathers. Many people had been torn by circumstances from their old moorings or had been enticed by opportunities for adventure and gain to travel far afield in quest of good fortune. In critical moments they found themselves far removed from the old supernatural helpers to whom they had formerly appealed. Time and distance, to say nothing of other impediments, rendered impracticable any hurried visit to some remote part of the world where one might seek help from the deities who had protected one's ancestors. There was a constantly increasing demand for gods who could aid a lone individual in all the varying conditions of life and in any quarter of the world.

The mobility of the population, with its diverse elements mingled at every important center, still further augmented the demand for gods to serve an individual. Peoples of different blood and varying racial heritages mingled together within the confines of a city, a village, the army, and even a single household. Some persons moved about voluntarily and others under the compulsion of necessity. The peace of the Empire, with good roads and a sea free from pirates, enticed merchants to seek far-distant markets. Soldiers, recruited from the far corners of the Empire, served in all parts of that world. When discharged from the army and granted their allotment of land, they became citizens in many places. Slaves also contributed extensively to the fusion of peoples. We have "nations in our household," said Tacitus, and the growing practice of manumission turned loose upon society a vast horde of freedmen who dispersed themselves everywhere over the Roman world in quest of more favorable opportunities for subsistence.

The heterogeneous character of the population demanded a great variety of cults if every person's necessities were to be met. The Greek or the Syrian slave in a Roman family could not be expected to find satisfaction for his distinctive religious needs by worshiping the Roman gods of his master and his mistress. It was essential to his happiness that he should continue to direct his quest for help to the type of divinity he had been accustomed to serve in the land of his birth. He must either transport his native gods to the place of his exile or find in his new home deities who could discharge functions he had been accustomed to associate with the operation of his father's gods.

The individual frequently confronted crises the like of which he had never met before. In his new mode of life there were fresh experiences for which his ancestral traditions provided no help. He must seek additional supernatural assistance among his new neighbors. In association with his companions he might be able to offer them some help from his heritages, while at the same time he sought from them a knowledge of other gods capable of ministering to his peculiar needs. Thus he might become a missionary for his ancestral faith and a seeker after a new supernatural assistance to be derived from the faith of his associates.

In this process of give-and-take, religion took on a stronger personal character. Cults that offered the individual an opportunity to secure blessing and protection through one's voluntary approach to the deity became most popular. Men coveted contact with supernatural powers whose help could be secured as a reward for the devotee's deliberate choice of the protecting divinity. This meant an assurance guaranteed by participation in initiatory rites open to every individual regardless of race or nation or social status. One approached the gods in a purely personal capacity. Individual initiative was rewarded by membership in a voluntary association of disciples bound to one another and to the deity by the proper performance of sacred ceremonies.

It was no accident that the type of religion commonly called the mysteries gained wide popularity in the Roman Empire. It was in just these cults that the largest opportunity was offered for the cultivation of personal experience in one's relations with the supernatural powers. To become a devotee of the mighty Isis or of the great mother-goddess Cybele, or even of the ancient Greek Demeter, meant that the individual voluntarily sought membership in the cult and underwent the preparatory discipline necessary for admission. The worshiper believed that his personal devotion to the gods was reciprocated by their personal interest in him and his welfare. He felt that he was under the protection of deities who were in full sympathy with mankind bcause they had shared with mortals the common experiences of life and death. Consequently, they were especially able to succor humanity in every hour of need.

The immense gain in the satisfaction and enrichment of personal experience made possible by the mystery religions can scarcely be overstated. The failure of the state cults to meet personal religious needs, which the social conditions of the time had emphasized, was probably the chief reason for the ultimate failure of official Roman religion to maintain itself with any degree of vitality in the later years of the Empire. Even though the government might be thought stable and eternal under the guardianship of the nation's mighty gods, the individual became ever more keenly aware of vicissitudes and crises in his personal experience from which the government offered him no protection. He needed divinities who, though perhaps unable to guide the destinies of a nation, could provide a realistic salvation for an individual both in this life and in the world beyond the grave.

In the ardor of his attachment to his new-found deities the devotee was often ready to claim for them not only power to help the individual, but a universality of operation that rendered the gods of the state practically useless. In the case of Isis, for example, whose worship had originally been connected with a specific sanctuary in Egypt, her disciples in Roman times were convinced that she exercised world-wide powers over all the concerns of society. No other god was needed for any of life's exigencies. They declared her to be the source and protectress of civilization, the guardian of mankind, and the eternal mistress of the cosmos.

No individual, however unfortunately circumstanced in Roman society, needed to go without the aid that supernatural beings were believed able to afford. Whether it was a question of physical health, of impoverished emotions, of degenerate character, or of fear for the future welfare of his soul, deities were believed to stand ready to give ample assistance if one personally put forth the necessary effort to place one's self into right relations with the higher powers. Certain of these gods specialized in one or another form of help, but so widely had the individual type of religion spread about the world that there was no place where the services of a great variety of such divinities were not available. Moreover, among Gentiles of that age not the least impropriety was felt in paying respect to many different gods. In fact, the more contacts one could make with the supernatural, the more happily and safely might one expect to live. The notion of a jealous god was a Jewish and a Christian concept which other people in the Roman world did not share. They desired to respect every divinity who came within their ken. And if the individual failed to realize to the full a sense of personal protection, it was not because there was not a sufficient number of deities available but rather because through some failure of his own he had not been successful in procuring the necessary divine assistance.

II

The quest for health was one of the most urgent personal demands made upon the deities by people living in the Roman Empire. Then, as now, the healing of disease was a problem lying very close to the heart of humanity. Sickness and death were the same hard facts of universal experience that they are today. Sanitation was bad and medical science inefficient. Wasting pestilences often carried away large numbers of the population, while less fatal sicknesses were a constant inconvenience and a source of unending anxiety. The physical afflictions of humanity were legion. There were diseases of the mind and of the body, internal and external, real and imaginary. This situation offered the divinities an exceptionally fine opportunity to show their power and to demonstrate their favor for their worshipers.

The Roman world was not totally given over to the superstitious treatment of disease, as though it were entirely an affair of the gods. The Greek philosophers had not ignored this very vital area of human experience. They proposed explanations regarding the cause of disease and suggested methods of treatment that tended to place the whole matter upon a

purely natural basis. Plato had interested himself in the subject, and his views were repeated over and over again by his
disciples in later times. He affirmed that sickness was simply
the result of derangement in the physical body. Perhaps
through improper action by the individual, or in consequence
of some accident over which one had no control, the constituent elements making up the body had been thrown into dis-
order. In that case the only proper remedy was to restore if
possible the original harmony. Mental diseases were also due
to the same causes. This was inevitable, since discord in the
body would invariably affect the well-being of the soul. Consequently, Plato proposed, as the best antidote for sickness,
education and a well-ordered life in order that the proper
balance might be restored in the elements making up the substance of the body and the constitution of the soul. Hence one
who engages in intellectual pursuits should also practice gym-
nastics in order to keep the limbs of the body in harmony with
the motions of the soul.

The medical practitioner seems to have been a well-known
figure among the Greeks in Plato's day. He used "burning,
cutting, drugging, starving" in his treatment of disease; and,
in general, Plato seems to have had a rather poor opinion of
Greek doctors. He placed much more confidence in a regimen
than in physic. He believed that nature herself was the best of
healers and that, as a rule, physicians were to be shunned, since
medicines tended rather to aggravate than to allay disease.

The Epicurean philosophy accounted for all sickness by
positing the existence of a particular kind of atom whose
proclivities remind one not a little of the modern germ. Just
as there were seeds of many things helpful to our life, so harm-

ful atomic bacilli flew about in the air ever ready to produce disease and death. Where they accumulated in large numbers, they disordered the atmosphere, and the air became infected. Thus "pestilences come either from without down through the atmosphere in the shape of clouds and mist, or else they gather themselves up and rise out of the earth when it is soaked with water and has contracted a taint, being beaten upon by unseasonable rains and suns."[1] Under these conditions the only sure way of escape from disease lay in avoiding contact with the infectious germs.

The Stoics viewed disease as an inescapable incident in the natural order of events, but they raised it above the level of mere naturalism and linked it with the will of an overruling providence. Now and then Zeus might use sickness as a means of punishing the wicked, but this was not the main purpose of affliction. Indeed, it often happened that the righteous were smitten quite as severely as sinners. It was thought not to have been the original purpose of the deity to make man subject to disease; but, in making a world that would be serviceable and beneficial to mankind, the creator had been compelled to allow for the possibility of sickness. Health and disease were necessary complements of each other. In constructing a human body in such fashion that it would serve the purposes of reason and utility, the head, for example, was necessarily fashioned of very small and thin bones. Yet a head thus constructed was easily broken. Similarly, other parts of the body when fashioned for efficiency were always liable to the possibility of derangement. Hence disease was an integral part of the rational order and should be borne with equanimity.

[1] Lucretius *Nature of Things* vi. 1090 ff.

Not everybody in the ancient world was able to acquire the philosopher's serenity in facing disease. To the vast majority ill-health appeared to be a calamity rather than a normal occurrence, and they eagerly sought relief from affliction. The physician was much in demand and was especially welcome when it could be supposed that he operated by supernatural power. But even persons like Pliny the Elder, to whom supernaturalism was distasteful, believed that an efficient physician could by experimentation and observation learn from nature herself methods of treatment and remedies for diseases that would restore an invalid to health.

The first man to take up the practice of medicine was said to have been Hippocrates, who was reputed to have learned the art from the great divine healer Asklepios. Legend accused Hippocrates of copying from the temple of Asklepios prescriptions which the god had given to invalids to cure their afflictions. Then Hippocrates burned the temple and began the practice of medicine on his own account. He attended invalids in their beds instead of requiring them, as had formerly been the custom, to visit some temple. Thus he became the founder of that branch of medical practice known as "clinics." Pliny remarks that "after this time there was no limit to the profits derived from the practice of medicine." From Greece the medical practitioner early migrated to Rome. A certain Archagathus was said to have visited Rome in the year 218 B.C. At first he was received favorably by the authorities and called *vulnerarius* ("healer of wounds"). But, on becoming better acquainted with his methods, the Romans named him *carnifex* ("executioner"). The scientific practice of medicine in the ancient world, while earnestly pursued by a few individuals, had not yet won universal recognition.

Among Jews and Christians the profession of physician was not always popular. The Chronicler remarked with evident disapproval that King Asa when sick did not seek health from Jehovah but went to the physician, with the result that the king soon "slept with his fathers" (II Chron. 16:12-13). But the writer of Ecclesiasticus advised that the physician be held in honor as one whom God has approved. Moreover, the Lord has created medicines out of the earth, and a prudent man will not treat them with disdain. It is very true that when sick one ought first to make things right with God and then call in the physician, for "verily the Lord hath created him" (38:1-15).

The early Christians concerned themselves little if at all with the practice of medicine as a natural art. Luke was remembered as "the beloved physician," whose companionship had been affectionately esteemed by Paul, but the apostle plainly indicated that for Christians the healing of disease was the proper task of religion. For Paul it was the risen Jesus whose therapeutic power equipped disciples with "gifts of healings," but in the next generation, when the Gospels were written, tradition represented Jesus in the role of a great physician during his earthly career. Henceforth the healing ministrations of Christianity were thought to be the only hope for the ills of humanity.

The therapeutic value of religion was an idea widely current among Gentiles before Christians appeared on the scene. If the new religion was to surpass its competitors, it must show itself equally competent in this field of activity, for the Gentiles were thoroughly habituated to the custom of seeking both the cause of disease and its cure in the realm of the supernatural. It was popularly assumed that there had been no sickness among men in their primitive ideal state until that unhappy day when Pandora lifted the lid from the fatal box. Since that day unwelcome diseases afflict mankind. They move silently through the air, Zeus having deprived them of a voice, and fill the world with woes.[2]

Often sickness was believed to be due to the anger of an avenging divinity. It was not uncommon for the superstitious Gentile to regard his bodily infirmity or the death of a relative as "plagues from god and assaults of the demon." Even the propriety of seeking remedial measures under such circumstances was sometimes questioned. Might not a patient who summoned a doctor appear to be fighting against the deity? Plutarch deplored the benighted condition of those who were so deluded as to push away the physician and exclaim in despair, "Let me alone to suffer my punishment, impious and accursed as I am, hateful to gods and to demons."[3] Among the Romans there was a prevailing belief that the gods, when disobeyed, punished men with bodily afflictions.[4]

That sickness was punishment for offenses against the deity was also a common Jewish notion. Adam and Eve because of their sins were supposed to have brought down the curse of pain on mortals. Jehovah's displeasure with the Egyptians had been the cause of the terrible plagues with which they had

[2] Hesiod *Works and Days* 90 ff.

[3] Plutarch *Superstition* vii (168C).

[4] E.g., Livy *History* ii. 36; ix. 29; xxv. 26; Tacitus *History* iv. 84.

been afflicted, but God had promised the pious Hebrews that he would "heal all their diseases" (Exod. 15:26). Among the Jews of the Dispersion the same type of belief prevailed. Philo said that one who neglected the sacred laws should be afflicted by diseases of the body which separately afflict and devour each limb and each part, and which also rack and torture one all over with fever and chills and wasting consumption and terrible rashes and scrofulous diseases and spasmodic convulsions of the eyes and putrefying sores and abscesses—to mention only a few items in Philo's list of punishments to be expected by the wicked.[5]

Christians followed the example of their Jewish and gentile predecessors in taking sickness to be a mark of divine displeasure. Before commanding a lame man to walk, Jesus had first announced the forgiveness of the victim's sins, and on another occasion he had admonished one whom he had healed to "sin no more lest a worse thing befall thee" (Mark 2:5–12; John 5:14). Paul saw in the sickness and death of certain members of the Corinthian community the chastening of the Lord for their improper observance of the Lord's Supper (I Cor. 11:30–32). But the notion of divine retribution was quite too narrow a basis on which to account for all sickness among Christians. Sometimes admittedly good people were themselves ill, and it followed that one must ascribe sickness to the activity of arbitrary evil powers who laid hold alike upon the wicked and the righteous. Paul believed that his personal infirmity was an affliction from Satan that God permitted for Paul's own good.

While individuals believed themselves to be the helpless

[5] *Curses* v.

prey of demonic agencies, who everywhere sought to afflict men with diseases and lay them low in death, the only genuinely effective remedies had to be found in the area of the supernatural. In the last resort it was the gods themselves upon whom the ancient man felt compelled to rely for deliverance from the ills to which human flesh is heir.

Both Greek and Roman legends were rich in stories of occasions when deities had served as physicians among men. When the inhabitants of a Greek city were dying of pestilence, it was Dionysus "who came with healing steps over the slopes of Parnassus." The people of Phocis cherished a shrine of Apollo whose oracles were thought to be a source of healing wisdom for all sick persons who sought help from the deity. Tradition narrated also that the mother-goddess Demeter on her first visit to Eleusis had found Triptolemus at the point of death but, by touching the mouth of the boy with her own, had restored him to life. Other divinities like Rhea and Hercules were called upon to "drive away disastrous maladies and dispel dire diseases to earth's remotest bounds."[6]

Among the multitudes of divine healers who served the Greeks, Apollo and his son Asklepios stood out most conspicuously. The reputation of Asklepios for health-giving ministrations rested on abundant tradition. While on earth he had cured all who came to him. Whether one was afflicted with ulcers, or suffered from wounds, or was a victim of summer's heat or winter's cold, an appeal to this healing god was never in vain. Some invalids he treated with charms, others were given soothing potions, to others he applied plas-

---

[6] See Sophocles *Antigone* 1142; Pausanias *Itinerary* x. 33. 5; Ovid *Fasti* iv. 537 ff.; and the *Orphic Hymns* xii. 14 ff., and xiv. 12 ff.

ters made from herbs, and on others he performed amputations. But, tempted by the promise of gold, once he had exerted his mighty skill beyond proper limits and had restored a dead man to life. This act brought his earthly career to an end, but in his new role as an immortal he continued to help all those who sought healing at his shrine.

In Roman times invalids from all parts of the world flocked to the famous sanctuary of Asklepios at Epidaurus in Greece, where healing was generously dispensed to hosts of suppliants. The lame, the blind, the paralytic—in fact, persons suffering from all kinds of maladies—found at this shrine healing for all their afflictions. Those who had been cured left behind ample testimony to the power of the god. If one were too ill or so unfortunately circumstanced that he could not make the journey to Epidaurus, some friend might carry his petition. He would then be answered either by a vision to the sick man in his own home or by a return message of information that would guide him to the recovery of his health. Also the god might be found at lesser shrines in many places around the Mediterranean long before Christian times.

The Romans were as confident as the Greeks had been that the health of mankind was a care of the gods. When a pestilence afflicted the community, the pious Roman doubled his devotion to deities. Among the many occasions when such help was sought, Livy reports a particularly striking incident. In the city of Rome itself a deadly scourge was raging. Disease spread so rapidly that the Senate ordered the people to make special supplication to the gods. Whole families, including the children, joined in the ceremonies, imploring the protection of heaven for the threatened city. One might see "prostrate maidens in every quarter, sweeping the temple with their hair and beseeching a remission of the divine displeasure and an extermination of the pestilence." Livy adds that conditions immediately improved, but he is in some doubt as to whether the favorable outcome was to be credited to the religious devotion of the people or to an improvement in the state of the weather. Whatever may have been Livy's doubts, certainly the populace accepted the legend without question.[7]

Early in their history the Romans learned that their native gods were unequal to the task of adequately protecting their health. As the population increased and the needs of the growing Empire became more acute, the Romans borrowed gods from the East to meet the new demands. By the beginning of the Augustan age both Apollo and Asklepios (Aesculapius) had become official protectors of the Roman health. In his famous *Saecular Hymn* Horace confirmed the Roman trust in Apollo, not only to drive away sickness from an individual whose frame might be racked by pain, but to insure for Rome in the future a happier day when the community would no longer experience devastating pestilences. For his kindly services as guardian of the public health, he was honored with a temple and became as truly a possession of the Romans as he had previously been of the Greeks. *Salutaris* and *medicinalis* were his fitting epithets in inscriptions.[8]

Asklepios early came to Rome to render divine assistance in the preservation of Roman health. He, too, had been imported in an hour of sore distress. A pestilence was raging, and

[7] *History* iii. 7.

[8] *Corpus inscriptionum Latinarum*, VI, 639; Livy *History* iv. 25. 3.

the local physicians were unable to stay the contagion. In desperation the authorities ordered that the Sibylline Books be consulted, and they advised that Asklepios should be brought from Epidaurus to Rome. In the form in which the story passed down in Roman tradition his coming was a tremendously momentous event in the history of the Roman people. Now they had a new divine guardian of health, who served not only the community at large but also every individual that sought his assistance. The new deity was as much concerned with healing the humblest suppliant as with warding off pestilence from the Empire. Even a blind soldier could confidently attest his gratitude to the god for restoring his sight by instructing him to anoint his eyes for three days with a salve made from the blood of a white cock mixed with honey. And a sick slave who had been left to die on the island in the Tiber where the temple of Asklepios stood enjoyed complete freedom from his old master when the deity had restored the slave to health.[9]

Healing gods from Asia and Egypt also migrated extensively about the Mediterranean. Sick persons had a wide choice among the divine physicians to whom they might appeal. Local divinities, like Sandan of Tarsus, still retained their reputation for curative power. Although in far-distant Sardinia, the man from Syria could enjoy the healing ministrations of the Phoenician Eshmun, as is attested by the dedication of a bronze altar by a certain Cleon in gratitude to the god who had "heard his voice and healed him."[10] The Phryg-

[9] *Corpus inscriptionum Graecarum*, No. 5980, 15 ff.; see also Livy *History* x. 47; Ovid *Metamorphoses* xv. 622 ff.; Suetonius *Claudius* xxv.

[10] *Corpus inscriptionum Semiticarum*, I, 143.

ian mother of the gods could be hopefully petitioned by sick persons in Greece as early as the time of Pindar.[11] When Alexander the Great was ill in Babylon, the temple of Serapis was thought to be the final court of appeal on the question of the prince's restoration to health. In the next century the cult of Serapis spread extensively about the eastern Mediterranean, where he was conspicuously a deity prone to afflict with sickness those who disobeyed his commands and to insure for his faithful devotees "the health of the body." From his home in Egypt the healing fame of Serapis penetrated to the limits of the Roman Empire, and, on account of his activities as a divine physician, he was often called Aesculapius by the Romans.

The Egyptian Isis enjoyed a similar reputation. Her curative powers were attested by numerous representations in her temples to be found at many places about the Mediterranean in the Augustan age. She was declared to have been the discoverer of medicines and therefore to take special delight in healing diseases. It was claimed that persons who had been pronounced incurable by the physicians had been restored to perfect health on appealing to the goddess. Other suppliants sought the aid of more transcendental divinities, like the seven gods guarding the world's axis and holding power over the lightning and the earthquake. They, too, were trusted to bestow "good health and soundness of body, strength of hearing and sight."[12]

When Christian missionaries entered the gentile world, preaching the healing power of their risen and heaven-exalted Lord Jesus, they found audiences well prepared to hear their

[11] Pindar *Pythian* iii. 77 ff.

[12] See text in A. Dieterich, *Eine Mithrasliturgie* (2d ed.), p. 14.

message. It was incumbent on Christians to make the most of this opportunity. They were confident that the power of the risen Jesus was superior to that of any demon or mightier divinity of gentile fame. They bore testimony to the power of Christ, not only through their own courage and enthusiasm as healers of disease in his name, but by recalling the story of his earthly career as a mighty wonder-worker before whom all demonic powers that tortured and afflicted men had trembled and fled. Christians were confident that Jesus had been even more effective in his ministrations to the sick than ever could have been the case with any Dionysus or Demeter or Apollo, or Asklepios or Isis or Serapis, or all of them combined. Jesus had excelled all others in restoring health to the sick and had surpassed all rivals in his power to restore the dead to life. Christians had no need for a natural science of medicine because they were confident that supernatural help had been made abundantly available for them through the mediation of their Great Physician.

III

An enduring government and a healthy body secured by the favor of heaven were accounted great blessings in ancient times. Yet many persons were keenly conscious of still another form of good quite beyond the reach of the average individual without divine assistance. The well-being of his spirit seemed of greater moment than the strength of his body or the stability of politics. Neither the permanence of the social order nor the continuance of physical health could insure the eternal welfare of his spirit when at last the inevitable hour arrived for the separation of his soul from the body and its earthly associations. It behooved him therefore while still in the body to seek help for the health of his soul.

The mental life of the ordinary individual must often have been one of much anxiety. The world was full of terrors, seen and unseen. The dangers, invisible though they might be, that threatened the human spirit were dreaded even more than were such calamities as earthquakes, pestilence, or like misfortunes more easily perceived by the physical eye. The inner life of feeling, with its interplay of emotions, seemed quite as real as more external phenomena, if not in fact the greatest reality with which one had to reckon. Dangers threatening the well-being of the spirit were only the more dreaded because less easily perceived by the eye of sense, or because they emanated from supernatural powers whose evil will could not be easily thwarted. The gravest concern of one's life was how to secure for the spirit a divine protection by which the immortal part of man could successfully evade or resist its enemies.

The soul had many foes. There were vast hordes of evil spirits that might work irreparable harm to an individual unskilled in the art of securing supernatural protection. They caused pestilences which from time to time carried off large numbers of people. It seemed proper also to make them responsible for those cosmic convulsions when the forces of good and evil had contended together for the control of the universe. There seems to have been a sinister feeling abroad that the demons had the first right to the human soul, which in its natural state was a normal object on which these evil powers preyed. Consequently, the great human struggle at the present moment was to ally one's self with the counteracting forces of good by which the soul might gain new strength for its perpetual combat with enemies.

Some men were nervously conscious of their helplessness amid the inexorable operations of cosmic forces. The world itself was a supernatural thing, whether one thought it to be dominated by the stars, under the compulsion of necessity, or ruled by the irresponsible goddess of fortune. Juvenal spoke for only a minority of his contemporaries when he remarked that "the only pathway to a life of peace is by way of virtue; if one has understanding, thou, Fortune, hast no divinity; it is we who make of thee a goddess and place thee in heaven." Most men feared the baneful goddess and despaired of their power to escape her buffetings until they had obtained assurances of protection by some superior divinity. They craved the experience of a Lucius who, when received into the cult of Isis, could say of Fortune: "Let her go now and rage with all her fury and let her seek some other object for her cruelty; for direful calamity has no power over those whose lives the majesty of our goddess (Isis) has claimed for her own service."[13]

Again, there were many persons who thought the physical body itself an enemy of the spirit. Plato's familiar saying that the body is the prison-house of the soul was never forgotten. This essentially Orphic teaching, that soul and body belonged to different spheres of existence, gave to man the uneasy feeling that his spirit was entombed in an evil body bent on chastising the spirit and dragging it down to closer union with matter. If the individual remained unaided by any power

[13] Apuleius *Metamorphoses* xi. 15; cf. Juvenal *Satires* x. 363 ff.

outside of himself in this unequal struggle between the imprisoned spirit and the evil body, death would bring liberty to the soul but would leave it in a condition so tarnished and impure that it might be forced to return again and again to a bodily habitation. Relief from this unfortunate fate could be secured only by calling to one's aid some new divine assistance in the present life.

Under these circumstances the deities of chief interest to many persons were those who could inspire a feeling of salvation realizable in the emotional experience of the individual. Immunity from evil demons and their machinations, whether in this world or in the world to come, could be attained only through the consciousness of union with some more powerful kindly divinity pledged to protect needy humanity. One turned to such a god as the only hope of deliverance from the indifferent or unkindly cosmic powers representing the vast organism that men today call the course of nature. The ancient man craved fellowship with a divine friend whose all-seeing eye and supernatural power could liberate the helpless individual from this heartless nexus of events. And if he were to realize any sense of victory over the impulses of the flesh, he felt that this could be accomplished only through the incoming of fresh divine energy to supplement the native force of his spirit in the unequal conflict.

The human spirit's quest for an experience of salvation did not remain unanswered. Long before Christianity arose, there were many gentile religions inviting those who felt the need of divine assistance for the inward man. The rites of the various mystery religions offered an especially good opportunity for the attainment of a new emotional experience readily interpreted as an effective acquisition of fresh divine power. The stimulation of the senses by music and processionals, the play upon the feelings attending various acts in connection with the rites of initiation, the pledge to secrecy solemnly imposed upon all the candidates, the wild orgies connected with some of the cults—all served to produce the desired emotional agitation. The necessity of presenting one's self voluntarily for membership, as well as the purifications and other preparatory acts, only heightened the effect. Everything that was done happened to one as an individual, and this strong emphasis on the personal relations between the devotee and his god gave precisely the sense of divine interest which alone could produce in needy humanity feelings of solace and satisfaction.

Initiation into the mysteries was likened to the experience of death itself. It filled one with terror but issued in triumph. The joy which persons felt on completing the process of initiation could fairly be compared with the joy in store for the soul when finally it would depart from the body and be purified for entrance into the state of immortal bliss. One might say that in the confidence experienced by the devotee he already passed from death unto life through the rites of initiation. Plutarch noted the close similarity between the two types of experience, and Apuleius described in the same imagery the feelings of Lucius on completing the ceremonies of admission into the cult of Isis. Well might one celebrate as his natal day that joyous hour when his initiation had been accomplished. Henceforth he was the possessor of a new life into which he had been born through participation in the rites of the mysteries. He could not soon forget his *natalem sacrorum*.[14]

Thoughtful people saw behind the transforming experience of initiation more than a mere display of physical feeling. It is very true that the mysteries perpetuated certain observances offensive to the finer tastes of cultured people in Roman times. Plutarch could not believe—and he could cite the ancient Xenocrates in support of his skepticism—that any god or good demon took pleasure in the buffoonery practiced in the Eleusinian processions, when people made wry faces and perpetrated coarse jests or resorted to blows and abusive and obscene language. He explained that these absurd performances were resorted to as a means of warding off demons, who were especially pleased by such conduct. If they were not given this satisfaction, they might work great harm. The boisterous doings were thus a kind of exorcism, "propitious and soothing acts for the purpose of turning away wicked spirits," in order that the more sacred rites to follow might not be contaminated. But when the demons had been driven off and the candidates came to the most solemn part of the ceremony, they conducted themselves in a very different manner. Now the clamor and rudeness of the initial ceremonies gave place to "profound silence and religious fear." A reverential quiet pervaded the place, while the initiates waited to hear the sacred discourse, the "holy word," from the lips of the priest, whose utterances were received with awe and gratitude.[15]

For men like Plutarch, disposed to reflect on the deeper

[14] Plutarch *Face in the Moon* xxviii (943D); *Concerning the Soul*, Frag. vi. 2; Apuleius *Metamorphoses* xi. 23.

[15] Plutarch *Isis and Osiris* xxvi (361B); *Cessation of Oracles* xiv (417C); *Progress in Virtue* x (81E).

meaning of the mysteries, the rites seem to have had a distinctly transcendental significance. They symbolized experiences of the deity that were full of meaning for mankind. The enemies of the mystery gods had been wicked demons, like Typhon, who slew Osiris, or the Titans, who tore Dionysus limb from limb; while the supernatural powers who had authorized the mysteries were the good demons. They had triumphed over their foes and through their victory insured salvation for their devotees. Pursuing this line of thinking, it was easy for the members of the mystery cults to believe that they were under the protection of divinities who had successfully engaged in a mighty cosmic struggle with the forces of evil. Typical of this sentiment are the words which the priest addressed to the new members of the Phrygian cult who had just witnessed the holy pantomime portraying the experiences of the deity: "Be of good courage devotees of the god who has been saved, for you too shall have salvation from troubles."[16]

The mysteries also gave a sense of deliverance from imprisonment in the physical body. The purgations preceding initiation, the fasts and ascetic practices often connected with the rites, and the emotional extremes of sorrow and joy were aids in the mortification of the flesh and ladders by which the spirit ascended to new heights of self-assurance. The imprisoned soul had now been given new wings by the grace of the deity whose very presence was felt within the individual. Freedom from the oppression of physical nature had been made possible by the acquisition of a new divine increment of

[16] Firmicus Maternus *Error of Profane Religions* xxii; see also Plutarch *Cessation of Oracles* xxi (421D) and *Isis and Osiris* xxvii (361D).

being to supplement the life of the spirit; men spoke of being born again, born unto eternity.[17] The spirit of man needed rejuvenation, and numerous gentile cults provided an answer to this common human quest.

IV

Christianity aimed to meet every religious need of the gentile world. As the Christian preachers became more familiar with the demands of their gentile contemporaries, they enlarged the definition and operations of their own faith to show that it covered the entire area of proper religious yearning. They had no sympathy with Epicurean naturalism and hardly more with Stoic self-sufficiency. On the contrary, they were of like mind with the more superstitious heathen who sought help for individual necessities in the sphere of the supernatural. But Christians greatly simplified the suppliant's program by alleging that there was only one source from which all valid assistance was to be derived. They declared that faith in Christ gave one full access to the supreme divine power adequate for all the varied needs of every person within the total population of the Roman Empire. Whether one sought protection from the machinations of evil spirits, deliverance from bondage to cosmic powers, or release of the spirit from its bodily imprisonment, Christianity boldly declared that membership in its communion would provide a satisfactory experience of salvation.

To the apostle Paul must be given the credit for first discovering that Christianity could be made to function as a new mystery religion more capable than any of its predeces-

---

[17] *Corpus inscriptionum Latinarum*, VI, 736 (510).

sors of yielding adequate supernatural assistance for the needy human spirit. On reaching Corinth, Paul made a wise decision when he determined not to make any further efforts to convey his message to Gentiles in the style of a philosophical argument such as he had attempted in Athens. The heathen populace wanted to hear about saviors who through their own heroic careers had opened up new ways of help for distressed individuals. They were prepared to be impressed by a vivid portrayal of "Jesus Christ and him crucified." The import of such language cannot have failed to arrest their attention the moment these words fell upon their ears.

In his doctrine of the believer's union with Christ, Paul expressed the basic idea of all mystery religions, in which an immediate experience of union with a divine hero who had triumphed over death insured for the believer a similar victory. The newly initiated individual had received into himself a divine increment of being that gave fresh strength to his feeble spirit. He had become a "new" man. He had no such difficulty as moderns sometimes feel in taking literally certain phrases in the Pauline letters. He could readily understand their meaning when the preachers of the new religion spoke of the necessity of becoming a "new creation," of being "born again," or of having "Christ in you the hope of glory." Experience in the rites of the mysteries had taught Gentiles to take the imagery of union with the deity in very realistic fashion. When Paul substituted Christ for their former heroes, they had no difficulty in understanding his meaning.

As interpreted by Paul, Christ assumed responsibility for insuring every type of salvation that had previously been credited to any or all gentile saviors. He redeemed men from the downward drag of the evil flesh, he protected them from the hostility of all demons, and he rescued them from their dreaded cosmic foes. By his death and exaltation to heaven he had become triumphant in every quarter of the spirit-world. He was superior to the demonic rulers of this present evil age. He had met "the principalities and the powers" in deadly conflict and had despoiled them of their authority. No sinister astral divinities, however cruelly they turned the wheel of fate, held any power over the destiny of the soul that had experienced union with Christ. All heroic saviors of the mystery cults had now been superseded by Christendom's Lord Jesus Christ.

CHAPTER VIII
THE DESTINY OF THE SOUL

EVERYONE in the ancient world believed man to be composed of at least two constituent parts—the body and the soul. There could be no question regarding the fate of the body. Even though kindly divinities might temporarily alleviate physical ills to save one from an untimely end, death was inevitable. The body was destined for final disintegration. Whether deposited in a grave and left to decay or burned to ashes on a funeral pyre, ultimately it became inanimate dust. From this stern fact of universal experience there was no escape.

A happier destiny was in store for the soul. Because of its more ethereal nature it was able to survive the decease of the body from which it had departed at the moment of death. How long it would retain consciousness, where its future dwelling might be, and what experiences awaited it in its new abode were questions that made a strong appeal to the imagination. They had long been a serious concern of Greeks, Romans, Egyptians, Jews, and other peoples making up the cosmopolitan population of the Roman Empire. Various opinions were current. Many persons found greatest satisfaction in resorting to popular notions inherited from their ancestors or borrowed from the traditions of their new associates in the syncretistic society of the times. Others attempted a

173

reinterpretation of tradition in the light of new intellectual interests, and a few ventured on a program of radical skepticism.

I

In a notable treatise *Concerning the Soul* Aristotle critically summarized the opinions of earlier Greek philosophers regarding the nature, essence, and attributes of the entity commonly called the soul. He quite ignored popular religious notions and concluded that even the views of the philosophers were untenable. What gave him chief offense was the disposition of his predecessors to make the soul too independent of the body. He drew a sharp distinction between soul (*psyche*) and mind (*nous*) and identified the former with the vital principle possessed by both man and animals. He affirmed that "nothing which has perception is without soul."

In formulating his positive definition of soul, Aristotle's point of departure was a distinction between matter and form, subject and attribute, each being viewed as a substantial fact. Matter exists, form exists, and the two exist together. Matter represents potentiality, while form gives it attributes and the capacity for actuality. Similarly, body and soul have to one another the relation of matter and form, the soul giving function, attribute, or self-realization to a body which has in it the potentiality of life, that is, to a body possessing organs. To take an analogy, if the eye were an animal, eyesight would be its soul, in default of which it would no longer be a living eye. While body and soul were each allowed a real existence, just as the wax and the imprint both exist, a disembodied soul was inconceivable. Hence the soul was not immortal.

Fortunately for the average man's peace of mind, the Aristotelian psychology had no popular champion in the Roman Empire. But there were active preachers of skepticism, disciples of Epicurus, who proclaimed with evangelistic zeal the mortality of the soul. Epicurus had been a rigid materialist, yet he had believed that every man had a soul. This constituent part of the human personality was assumed to be composed of very fine and delicate particles of matter infusing and giving life to the coarser material of the visible body. But the atoms of which the soul was composed were thought to be so fiery, ethereal, and vaporous in character that they no longer held together when released from the body. After death the soul of the individual immediately perished, its atoms being reabsorbed into the great mass of primeval matter whence they had originally come. While this atomic substance endured eternally, the individual soul lost its identity at the moment of death, when its particles were dispersed even more rapidly than the atoms of the body.

Epicurean teaching regarding the soul was inspired by a desire to deliver man from the fears which beset him in this life as he meditated on what might await him in the world beyond the grave. By proving that the soul perished immediately upon leaving the body, the Epicurean thought that he was conferring a great blessing upon the human race. All fear of death would be abolished by removing the dread of future punishment. The Roman poet Lucretius vigorously declared that no man need fear any such punishments as were recounted in the Greek fables. It was only a diseased imagination that had created the picture of a Tantalus eternally tortured by the menace of a huge stone suspended above his head. Nor was there any Tityus with a carcass sprawled over nine acres while vultures continually tore at his liver. Sisyphus, vainly endeavoring to roll a huge marble block to the top of a hill, was also a pure fiction. Cerberus and the Furies, the wheel of Ixion, and Tartarus of the flaming throat were things "which nowhere are, nor sooth to say can be."[1]

In the next century Pliny the Elder also vigorously denied belief in the immortality of the soul. He insisted that all of man, soul and body alike, passed into oblivion at death, even as it had been without existence before birth. It was only vanity and self-deception on the part of man that inspired him to project himself into the future. Thus he had been deluded into believing that his soul would be immortal, or he had adopted the doctrine of transmigration of souls, or again had pictured for himself a life among the shades below, where departed spirits would receive worship from people who still lived on earth. Pliny impatiently exclaimed: "What madness it is to suppose that life is to recommence after death..... This pleasing delusion and this credulity quite cancel that chief good of human nature, death, and as it were double the miseries of him who is about to die by anxiety as to what is to happen to him thereafter." Man's more sensible procedure would be to remember that previous to his earthly existence he had been utterly unconscious and the same blissful oblivion awaited him after his life on earth came to an end.[2]

The happy oblivion to follow death was a theme often repeated in popular Roman literature, and many Roman epitaphs are famous for their jaunty treatment of the future life.

---

[1] Lucretius *Nature of Things* iii. 978 ff.

[2] Pliny *Natural History* vii. 55(56).

It is true that these inscriptions may sometimes record the witticisms of survivors rather than the serious views of the departed, but apparently it was felt to be entirely appropriate to make the deceased declare that he had passed into the never ending sleep of nonexistence. His life on earth had been a brief interlude between two eternities of absolute nothingness. One favorite epitaph ran thus: "I was not, I was, I am not, I care not." The living were admonished to cultivate the carefree life and enjoy sensation while it was still possible. Sentiments like the biblical "eat, drink and be merry, for tomorrow we die" recur time and again. Undoubtedly, Epicurean materialism was thought by some persons a veritable gospel worthy to be practiced during one's lifetime and to be paraded on one's tombstone after death.

Stoic philosophy had hardly more to offer in the way of personal hope for the future than had Epicureanism. Stoicism taught the immortality of the soul but allowed the individual little or no opportunity to enjoy future blessings in his own right. Every man's soul was, as it were, a piece of the great world-soul, or rational force, pervading the universe. This divine fire was resident in the body from the moment of birth and imparted the power of reason to the living man. With death the soul left the body to be reabsorbed into the primal ethereal substance from which it had come. Like a drop of water returning to the sea, the spirit of man passed out into the vast ocean of soul stuff. Buoyed up by this faith in the divine constitution and destiny of the soul, the Stoic had no fear of death. All souls were divine by nature and all returned home to god.

There was no room in the Stoic program for either punishment or reward on any such extensive scale as was provided in the popular mythology of the Greeks and the Romans. The Stoic speaker in Cicero's dialogue on the *Nature of the Gods* remarks: "Where can we find any old woman so silly as to believe the ancient stories of the horrors of the world below?" And Seneca declared that "the tales which make the world below terrible to us are merely poetic fiction, for death restores us to the peaceful rest in which we lay before we were born."[3]

Even those Stoics who allowed for a period of conscious personal immortality after death could not promise any hope beyond the great world conflagration to issue in the dissolution of all forms of being and a return of the world-substance to its primitive fiery state. At most, personal immortality could be of only limited duration. In the end a great catastrophe awaited the whole world when all nature would perish, the stars would be dashed together, and all the lights of the universe which now shine at regular intervals in their apportioned parts of the heavens would then blaze up in one common conflagration. The elements of the earth would all be dissolved or entirely destroyed in order that all might be created anew in innocence, with no remnant of the old order left to tutor men in vice. "A single day," says Seneca, "will see the burial of all mankind. All that the long forbearance of fortune has produced, all that has been reared to eminence, all that is famous and all that is beautiful, great nations, all will descend into the one abyss and will be overthrown in a single hour."[4]

---

[3] *Dialogues* vi. 19. 4; cf. Cicero *Nature of the Gods* ii. 2. 5.

[4] *Dialogues* vi. 26; *Natural Questions* iii. 29; Cicero *Nature of the Gods* ii. 46: cf. Pliny *Natural History* ii. 107(111).

Disciples of Plato were in a better position to satisfy the current demand for evidences of the soul's immortality. Under the influence of Orphic belief in the transmigration of souls, Plato had contended for the pre-existence of the individual soul and its survival after death. Resorting to mythological imagery, he had pictured the soul in the likeness of a charioteer whose car was drawn by two winged horses, the spirit and the appetites. When perfect and fully winged, the soul soared upward, while the imperfect soul lost its pinions and finally fell to earth. The manner in which it ordered its career while in the flesh determined its future destiny. At death it returned to the other world out of which it had come to receive its rewards for the deeds done on earth according as they had been evil or good. In the course of time the soul was compelled to resume its existence on earth. Only the few who had reached the climax of perfection or vice remained permanently in heaven or in hell. The great majority returned to earth for another trial, in order that they might have an opportunity to redeem themselves by correct living. After passing through the necessary reincarnations and the intermediate periods of retribution, they attained to a life of eternal blessedness. The soul that had dwelt three times in a philosopher was thereupon released from the necessity of further embodiments.

Plato's arguments for belief in immortality continued to be repeated by successive generations of disciples all through the period of the Roman Empire, but pure Platonism offered scarcely more popular satisfaction than did Stoic or Epicurean teaching. As a matter of fact, the Platonic view might make the individual far more uncomfortable. Even though the soul did survive the body, the outlook for the ordinary man was rather hopeless. His future well-being lay in his own hands and was not the care of any supervising divinities. The soul determined its own destiny. If it lost its wings through a bad choice, it had to win them again by severe self-discipline. The vulgar herd, as the philosophers were accustomed to designate men unschooled in the wisdom of the day, preferred to trust their religious traditions handed down in the teachings of the cults.

II

The speculations of the philosophers regarding immortality did not greatly concern the common people in the Roman Empire. Even many of the educated favored a form of belief indefensible on the strict grounds of reason and logic. Epicurean doubt might be loudly affirmed, but its advocates were more vociferous than numerous. Stoic apathy satisfied only the hardy-minded who, when brought face to face with death, often found it possible to adopt Platonic and Orphic notions or to resort to the beliefs of some mystery cult. Relative to the total population of the Roman world at the beginning of the present era, probably the number of persons who did not hold some form of belief in immortality was small. The ridicule of the satirists and the zeal of the skeptics were not directed at imaginary opinions. The popular foibles on which these writers traded had to be real in order to be profitable. The great mass of the population still held to traditional belief in the continued existence of the soul after its departure from the body.

From very ancient times the Greeks had been much interested in the destiny of the soul. The survival of the individual after death was believed to have been proved by many an experience of the living who in dreams had been visited by the spirits of the departed. Achilles' well-known vision of the deceased Patroclus is typical. The immortal part of the hero dwelt beneath the earth in a quiet, shadowy, uneventful place, if his friends had laid him to rest with fitting funeral rites.

Many stories were told of a restless spirit's return when the deceased had not been properly buried and consequently had not been furnished with the necessary counterpart to the body in the world of the shades. Often, too, it felt a lack of clothing or other adornment that should have been burned on the funeral pyre in order to provide it with a suitable wardrobe for its new abode. Once Periander, the tyrant of Corinth, sought advice from the spirit of his deceased wife, but she refused to help him until she was supplied with some new clothes fit to wear in the stylish society of the ghosts. When there was a great festival at Corinth, where all the ladies were attired in their best, Periander ordered them to remove their garments, which he forthwith burned in his wife's honor, this being the prescribed means of sending finery to the lower world. After this he made a second appeal to his wife, who then answered him according to his wishes. At other times it might be only the lack of a single slipper that would bring a ghost back to earth. But when a wife appeared in a vision to her husband, telling him where the slipper was to be found, he immediately burned it and thus laid the ghost.[5] The ancient Greeks knew that their dead friends still lived, separated from the scenes of their former existence by a thin partition between this world and the lower regions. In support of this belief one could cite numerous occasions when

[5] Herodotus *History* v. 92; Lucian *Liar* xxvii.

the deceased had returned to show themselves to their friends, to make known their wants, or to comfort the bereaved.

Among the Romans there was the same primitive belief that the ghosts of the dead abode underground and that their continued existence had often been proved by apparitions. When proper attention from the living was not forthcoming, they might seriously menace the well-being of those still on earth. That the departed were in need of food was recognized by the Romans as well as by the Greeks. In performing burial rites, the pious Roman offered "as sacrifices for the dead bowls foaming with warm milk and goblets of the sacred blood." It was in accordance with this ancient custom that the mother of Augustine, devout Christian though she was, used to deposit cakes and bread and wine at the shrines of the martyrs.[6]

The possibility of the soul's coming-forth from its tomb, or from the lower regions, to visit the scenes of its former activities was a constant menace to the Roman's peace of mind. There were several days in the year when he conducted religious rites designed particularly to satisfy the needs of the deceased. The festival of Parentalia in honor of one's dead relations, followed by the feast of All Souls (Feralia), was observed with great diligence, otherwise angry spirits would wreak vengeance on the living. Again, the Lemuria in the month of May were designed especially to conciliate and appease ghosts. It was a husband's fear of unfriendly visits from his deceased wife that prompted the inscription: "O dearest, spare thy husband I implore thee, spare him, that for many years longer he may continue to bring thee sacrifices and garlands and fill the lamp with fragrant oil."

[6] Vergil *Aeneid* iii. 66 ff.; Augustine *Confessions* vi. 2.

Experience with haunted places had similar evidential value. Ghosts often made places uninhabitable for mortals, especially when the spirit was that of one who had been violently killed or not buried with proper ceremony. At the time of Caligula's death his body had been taken privately to the Lamian Gardens, where it was hastily and only partially burned and remained carelessly covered over with earth. Thereafter the keepers of the gardens were frequently disturbed by apparitions, and not a single night passed without some terrible alarm in the house where Caligula had been slain. But finally the house was destroyed by fire and the sisters of Caligula, on returning from banishment, completed his obsequies. Thus his ghost seems ultimately to have been laid in peace. Plutarch's Roman readers would fully sympathize with the belief still current at Chaeronea that people in the neighborhood of the bath where Damon had met a violent death sometimes still saw specters and heard alarming sounds.[7]

Propertius in one of his elegies described an incident in support of the popular faith in immortality. He reported a vision granted to him by the deceased Cynthia soon after her funeral. He remarked upon the fact that she had the same hair and the same eyes on which he had looked when she was laid out for burial. He noted that her dress was scorched and clung to her side and the fire had destroyed the gem she generally wore on her finger. When she came from the lower world, the waters of the river of forgetfulness had washed her lips, and consequently she could not relate her experiences in the nether regions; yet she lived once more after the manner of her former earthly self. While this imagery was undoubtedly a

[7] Suetonius *Caligula* lix; Plutarch *Cimon* i.

highly poetical creation of the author, it was nevertheless true to popular belief in the survival of the human spirit. Propertius himself was thus convinced that "there are then such things as spirits, death does not end all, but the lurid shade overcomes and escapes the funeral pyre."[8]

III

Among both Greeks and Romans the earliest form of thinking about the future life placed relatively slight stress on the notion of individuality. It was the group life rather than the career of the individual that was uppermost in thinking, and the lower world rather than the sky was still the common abode of all deceased persons. These primitive notions never completely disappeared among the populace, although in later times they were extensively supplemented by new conceptions better suited to the type of social experience characteristic of the new imperial age. By the beginning of the Christian Era three new notions had clearly emerged. The vague imagery of mass immortality had given place to the more vivid portrayal of a future for the individual soul. There was also a livelier interest in rewards and punishments. In the third place, there was a growing disposition to transfer the abode of the blessed from the underworld to the realm of the stars, while the lower regions were reserved for evildoers.

When greater stress was placed on personal relations between the worshiper and the deity, there soon developed a keener sense of individual responsibility for the future welfare of the soul. The personal relations between a man and his god, true of life in the present, were thought to carry over into the

[8] *Elegies* v. 7. 1.

world beyond, and this idea stimulated interest in future rewards and punishments. Since it was the mystery religions
that met most widely the individual needs of the common
people in the Roman Empire, these cults were chiefly responsible for the rise of new ideas regarding the future life.
Among the Greeks the mysteries of Demeter, the Bacchic
rites, and Orphism had indeed at a comparatively early date
made their influence felt in this general direction. In Roman
times their teachings circulated more widely about the Mediterranean and were augmented by other mystery cults in
which the notion of immortality occupied a prominent place.

The hope of future bliss nourished by the mystery religions
was not of the philosophic type. They did not attempt to prove
immortality by argument. Belief was based on revelation
rather than on reason. The ecstasy experienced in the rites was
proof of the soul's capacity for enjoying communion with the
deity. Furthermore, since the gods revered in these cults had
themselves died and triumphed over the grave, they were able
to insure their devotees a similar privilege. In the rites of
initiation the soul had already experienced a foretaste of
future bliss. But those persons who remained outside the cult
would miss the blessings which the future held in store for
believers and would be doomed to an eternal life of misery.
One's present status before the divinity would endure beyond
death. Those who already enjoyed the assurance of salvation
would be happy in the world to come, while those who neglected the possibility of securing this divine favor in the present had no hope of being able to correct their error in the land
beyond the grave.

As a matter of fact, the Greek mystery religions had made a

significant contribution toward the formation of Plato's doctrine of immortality. He was often critical of their practices, and as a philosopher he rejected many of their beliefs. He advanced philosophical arguments to prove the immortality of the soul, while the devotees of the mysteries relied on emotion and faith supported by revelation. Yet Plato was ready to concede that the founders of these religions "had a real meaning and were not mere triflers, when they intimated in a figure long ago that he who passed unsanctified and uninitiated to the world below will live in a slough, but that he who arrives there after initiation and purification will dwell with the gods."[9] Thus far Plato could agree with popular faith, but he would substitute for the initiatory rites of the mysteries an acquaintance with the wisdom of the philosophers. That would make one the truly initiated and purified person who could be sure of a blessed hereafter.

Also among the Romans, even as early as the time of Cicero, the mysteries were reputed to be especially valuable for their teachings about immortality. All through the early imperial age their significance in this respect increased. Long before the Christian preachers appeared on the scene the advocates of the mysteries had been able to say to their hearers that trust in the divinities whom they preached would insure for one a happy life in the world beyond the grave. Even better-educated persons often sought comfort from this source when they felt the end of life to be drawing near or when overtaken by the death of a loved one. This was Plutarch's last resort when he sought to console his wife after the death of their young daughter. To the arguments for immortality which he

[9] *Phaedo* 69.

derived from other sources, he added a reference to the mysteries of Dionysus. Ultimately he trusted the religious symbols displayed in those sacred rites to convince the bereaved mother that not only the god himself but also the child of his devotees survived in the world to come.[10]

More specific information about the status of the individual after death was also available. In Greece the expectation of rewards and punishments had received much stimulus from Orphic and Pythagorean teaching. Orphism, as everyone knows, had laid great emphasis on the contrast between soul and body, the latter being inherently evil while the former was by nature divine. On account of sin committed in a previous state the soul was imprisoned in the body both for the sake of punishment and to provide an opportunity for improvement under discipline. In the lower world after death the soul experienced further catharsis before it entered upon another incarnation. By this process, continuing until the guilt of the soul had been entirely removed, it repaired at last to its divine home to enjoy eternal blessedness. This type of teaching, associated with the Dionysiac mysteries and promulgated in its philosophical form by the Pythagoreans, had largely influenced Plato.

The possibility of blessedness carried with it also the menace of punishment. Under the influence of Orphic imagery the contrast between the destiny that awaited good and evil souls, respectively, became greatly accentuated during the imperial age. Art as well as mythology served to depict the future state of punishment. One of the characters in Plautus' *Captives* remarked that he had frequently seen pictures of the torments

[10] *Consolation to His Wife* x (611D); cf. I Cor. 7:14.

inflicted in the lower world, but he believed that nothing could ever happen there equal to his experiences in the stone quarries. Pausanias described a famous painting by Polygnotus in the clubroom at Delphi in which the artist visualized the tortures of Hades with the explicit purpose of encouraging men to be pious. There is a vast amount of mythological scenery rich in suggestions of the soul's immortality available today in museums of Greek and Roman antiquities. Sometimes happiness, sometimes wretchedness, is symbolized in these representations. Frequently they have for their theme some god's or hero's triumph over death, thus implying a similar destiny for mortals who, if unsuccessful in their struggle, must surely face an unhappy fate.

In earlier phases of thinking both the good and the bad had been assigned their respective abodes in the lower world, but in the imperial age there was an increasing tendency to adopt astral notions which had come in from the East. Now it was possible to transfer the dwellings of the dead, and particularly of the righteous, to heaven. The soul was said to partake originally of the nature of the stars and hence its final home was the ethereal regions. Persons who were inclined toward fatalism even imagined that the destiny of the soul was ruled by the stars and that the entire earthly career of a newborn child could be read beforehand by one wise enough to discern the signs of the heavens. But whatever might be thought about the power of the stars over the living individual, one readily believed that after death the fiery ethereal spirit returned to its home in the upper regions. It now seemed fitting to transfer the abodes of the righteous dead to heaven, leaving the whole of the nether regions to the wicked.

Moreover, astral thinking had little interest in a place of torment. Since extensive provisions were made for the purification of souls on their way from earth to heaven, the infernal regions were no longer greatly needed. This is not to say that the place of torment vanished from the imaginations of the great mass of the people. One ought rather to say that those educated persons who had taken offense at the crude imagery of ancient Greek and Roman eschatology now found a way of escape other than that of Epicurean skepticism. They could, as some moderns are wont to do, abandon the notion of hell and retain the imagery of heaven. But the uncultured felt no such drive toward modernism.

In the case of an illustrious individual the ascension of the soul to heaven was a magnificent phenomenon. Of Julius Caesar, for example, it was said that his departed spirit assumed the form of a comet visible for seven days after his decease. Likewise the soul of the great Pompey, even though his body had gone down to ignominious defeat with the fall of the Republic, "could not rest in the glowing embers, nor could a few ashes contain that mighty shade. He sprang forth from the fires and leaving the body beneath, which the flames as yet had but half devoured, rose to the vault of heaven." He soared aloft to those regions "where heavenly bodies are at home, and where dwell spirits that are most akin to divinity, whose burning virtue kept them pure in life and brought them to the everlasting spheres."[11]

The souls of more ordinary mortals experienced a purification as they passed through the lower spheres to the regions on high. Plutarch in his interesting treatise on the face in the

---

[11] Lucan *Pharsalia* ix. 1 ff.

moon details the process by which the soul attained to astral purity. Following Aristotle's analysis, Plutarch holds man to be composed of body (*soma*), soul (*psyche*), and mind (*nous*). At death the body is left behind and returns to earth from which it came. The combined souls and minds mingle in the air for a time, suspended between the earth and the moon. The wicked are tormented in this intermediate space, but the virtuous finally gain a foothold on the moon. In the course of time the mind is liberated from the soul by a second death. The soul, left behind on the moon out of whose substance it was originally formed, goes back to the moon as body does to earth, while the mind, which is the truly immortal part, passes on to its native home in the sun.

This new theology, which transported both Hades and the Elysian Fields to the regions of the heavens, and made intellect superior to both body and soul, never displaced the older way of thinking. Greek and Roman literature continued to abound in descriptions of the nether regions where the wicked were punished in a place of torment and the righteous received their happy reward. Wide credence was given to a great variety of stories recounting visits of men to the lower world, where they had obtained detailed knowledge of the doings in those regions and had returned to encourage and admonish their contemporaries.

Visions of sinners in distress served to warn the living of the fate awaiting them unless they regulated their lives according to worthy standards of righteousness. A striking example was the story of Thespesius of Soli, a very wicked youth who was granted a three days' release from the body to pay a visit to the lower world. There he acquired a knowledge of the future that inspired him after his return to alter completely his previous manner of life. He came back thoroughly convinced that in the world to come the wicked would be subjected to hideous tortures. He describes some of the sights that he had been permitted to behold in the place of punishment. Even his own father was among the victims. There were welts on his soul, and gashes and scars, imposed because he had once poisoned several of his guests in order to confiscate their property. In his lifetime he had never divulged this secret, but it had been easily discovered in the lower world by the marks which the crime had left upon his naked soul. Punishment was now inevitable. Forms of punishment varied according to different sorts of crimes. Demons were employed extensively in the work of torture. Sometimes they immersed the soul in a lake of boiling gold and then, pulling it out, threw it suddenly into another lake of frigid lead. Next they dragged it over rough masses of iron. This program was repeated over and over again while the victims howled in agony as they remembered what they had already endured and cringed in terror before what awaited them at the hands of their relentless tormentors.

The satirical Lucian treated this favorite theme in a lighter vein, but he was well aware that, in dealing with the subject, he easily found himself on common ground with his audiences. Century after century it continued to be a popular belief that the soul was immortal and that through the reported visions of seers and the repeated stories of literature men knew the fate awaiting the wicked and the blessings in store for the righteous. There was a direct line of succession in such imagery right down through the ancient world from Homer,

Pindar, Plato, Vergil, Plutarch, and Lucian to Dante and Milton.[12]

IV

When Christian preachers began their missionary activities among the Gentiles, they were compelled to face the already widely discussed question of the destiny of the soul. But Christians had a ready answer. Belief in the immortality of the soul was an essential conviction with them from the very outset. At first they were inheritors of Jewish views on this subject, a fact that necessitated some important readjustments in their thinking as the new religion passed from Palestine into the gentile world.

In earlier Hebrew imagery comparatively little attention had been given to the destiny of the individual soul. But by the beginning of Christian times Jews had very definitely adopted belief in the immortality of the individual, with suitable rewards and punishments awaiting him in the future life. Yet Jewish thinking differed from Greek and Roman in one important respect. The Jews insisted on the necessity of a bodily resurrection before the soul would be able to attain to its final beatific state. The ultimate determination of the soul's destiny awaited the coming of a day of judgment, when the body would be revived and reinhabited by the spirit. The individual, thus once more complete, would be assigned an appropriate place in the new order of existence. The righteous would enter a paradise of delight, while the wicked would go to a place of torment.

[12] See Homer *Odyssey* xi. 566–631; Plato *Republic* 614 ff.; Vergil *Aeneid* vi. 625 ff.; Plutarch *Whom God Is Slow To Punish* xxii ff.; Lucian *Dialogues of the Dead* xxx; *Menippus* xiv ff.; *True History* xxxi; *Liar* xxiv–xxv.

The earliest Christian preachers endeavored to convert Gentiles to the Jewish way of thinking. Christians asserted that the end of the world, accompanied by a final judgment, was to be expected at an early date. The day of the Lord was at hand, when Jesus would descend from heaven, raise the dead, execute judgment, and inaugurate the Kingdom of God in a miraculously renovated Palestine. But this eager hope for a catastrophic end of the world, to be attended by a resurrection of the dead, remained year after year unfulfilled. Moreover, the resurrection of the physical body had never been an integral part of gentile belief in immortality. Consequently, Christians were soon confronted by the necessity of making some readjustments in their thinking regarding the destiny of the soul. Had they adhered rigidly to their original Jewish type of thinking, they could not have pictured any very vivid realization of either rewards or punishments after death until the resurrection had been accomplished and Jesus had returned to earth to enact the judgment. While Christians were slow to admit that resurrection and judgment were unimportant, they did find it possible to project both of these items a long way forward into the future, and in the meantime they adopted the more distinctively gentile belief that the departed spirit freed from the body realized immediately after death the blessings stored up in heaven for the righteous or the torments of the underworld that awaited unrepentant sinners.

Christians troubled themselves little if at all with problems distinctive of the philosopher. They felt no necessity for positing the pre-existence of the soul in order to hold, in Platonic fashion, that belief in immortality could be logically justified. Their conviction, like that of the gentile populace, rested on a supernaturally attested tradition. Visions of departed friends, or sights that had been witnessed by favored seers who had been permitted to gaze upon the place where the dead dwelt, were chiefly relied on for information about the future state. The Corinthians were well prepared to give heed to Paul's argument in proof of the immortality of the spirit when he cited the reappearance of Jesus after death in support of this belief. For Paul this fact was evidence also of a bodily resurrection, but the Corinthians, being Gentiles, not unnaturally found considerable difficulty in following Paul's reasoning on this point. A Greek could ask many embarrassing questions about what sort of body one might expect to acquire in the event of a resurrection. To many a Gentile it would in reality have seemed a calamity to force the soul once more to be shut up in the prison-house of a physical body.

The value of individual religious experience in shaping the future destiny of the human spirit now received in Christianity an emphasis distinctly gentile in its character. Those persons who had been accustomed to believe that through union with the deity they could even in this life anticipate the beatific state of the soul after death were informed that a similar type of experience was possible through entrance into the Christian society, where one realized at the very moment of initiation a consciousnss of union with the triumphant Christ. Henceforth the disciple felt assured that his title to immortality rested, not on any inherent necessity in the nature of the soul itself, or on his personal efforts to live a life intrinsically worthy of happy rewards, but on the power and favor of the deity in whom he had placed his trust. In Christianity, as in the cult of Dionysus or Demeter or Isis, an assurance of immortality was an integral part of present religious experience. Because the savior lived on in glory, his followers would find abundant entrance into the abodes of the blessed (John 14:19).

When Christians undertook to portray the respective states of the wicked and the righteous after death, they were not at the outset very well equipped with imagery for this purpose. Their eyes had been fixed on a coming day of judgment after which rewards would be meted out in proper fashion to saints and to sinners. The state of the departed dead previous to the day of judgment had not been given serious attention. But with the shift of thinking necessitated by the spread of the new religion to the gentile world, more consideration had to be given to the state of the soul immediately after death. The imagery of a Hebrew Sheol retired into the background and was superseded by the gentile notion that immediately after death the saints entered a blissful paradise, while sinners went directly to a place of punishment.

When portraying the tortures due to the wicked, Christians had two sources from which to draw their imagery. In their Jewish heritage they found vivid pictures of the afflictions to be imposed on unrepentant sinners after the great judgment. On the other hand, their gentile environment supplied them with a similar array of tortures prepared in Hades for the unrighteous. At this point Orphic imagery was particularly suggestive, and Christians were able to appropriate a considerable amount of this lower-world paraphernalia. Such documents as the Apocalypse of Peter show rich borrowings from earlier gentile speculations. In this narrative the disciples are given not only a vision of the delightful abodes of the blessed but a more detailed view of the frightful tortures of the wicked portrayed in a fashion already familiar to us from descriptions found in Homer, Vergil, and Plutarch. Punishments are allotted in accordance with specific crimes, and the horrors of the scene are typically Orphic.

In describing the delights of heaven, Christians at first employed the Jewish imagery of an ideally purified life in Palestine. Their task in this respect was rendered comparatively simple through the appropriation of distinctively Jewish pictures of the rewards due the righteous after the day of judgment. But, with the spread of the Gospel to gentile lands, new elements gradually entered into the Christian picture. Very soon features appear that were derived from popular Greek and Roman thinking. Both in literature and in art early Christianity drew freely upon the newly available heritages furnished by its gentile converts. The beatific scenery of the Elysian Fields was reproduced in Christian settings. Christians lent their support especially to the already prevailing tendency to transfer the abodes of the blest from the lower regions to the starry heavens. The Christian paradise was not beneath the earth but in the sky, whither the heathen paradise had already been carried by gentile theologians like Seneca and Plutarch.

So far as Christianity's capacity to provide suitable rewards and punishments for individual souls was concerned, it no longer greatly mattered whether the return of Christ to awaken the dead and set up the day of judgment was to occur tomorrow or centuries hence. This originally Jewish imagery continued to hold a conspicuous place in the dogma of the church, but it was supplemented by a vivid portrayal of the dead saints' immediate participation in future bliss, while deceased sinners went at once to their place of torment. The mansions in the sky, which Jewish thinking had reserved for God, the holy angels, and a few heroic human figures like Moses, Enoch, Elijah, and Christ, were now opened in gentile fashion to all righteous souls. The Hebrew Sheol no longer housed the ancient worthies. With more than Herculean power or Orphic persuasion, Christ had descended to Hades to rescue the spirits in prison (I Peter 3:19; 4:6). Henceforth the murky darkness of Sheol was lighted up by the lurid glare of the eternal fires of torment. Jewish imagery, depicting afflictions to be visited on sinners after judgment, and gentile pictures of present agonies experienced by sinners in the lower world were blended into one ghastly array of fiendish tortures awaiting every soul that passed the gates of death without an experience of the redeeming power of Christ.

CHAPTER IX
THE SUPPRESSION OF THE MIND

MEN of culture in antiquity were much given to admiration of the intellect for its contributions to civilization. However much the gods might do to help mankind, the human mind itself was thought capable of bestowing great benefits on mortals. By the rigidity of its operations men learned to be philosophers, and unstinted praise of philosophy was a favorite theme with all persons who accounted themselves intelligent. Cicero had declared philosophy to be the parent of all the arts and the only safe guide for life; it was she who had taught justice, modesty, and culture of soul. In the opinion of Lucretius worldly possessions, kingly glory, and noble birth were insignificant in comparison with the blessings of philosophy and her power to dispel darkness from the human soul. Stoics looked to her for the guidance that made men wise and good. The emperor Marcus Aurelius, reflecting on the perplexing uncertainties of life, had declared philosophy to be the only safe guide for one to follow; and Seneca had thought her to be far superior to all other learned arts, in that it was her peculiar task to guide men in matters of conduct and to teach them the nature and power of heaven.

Philosophy was said to be the only adequate remedy for the aberrations and diseases of the human mind and to constitute the principal item in all education. Under her guidance the child learned to worship the gods, to honor parents, to reverence elders, to respect the laws, to obey rulers, to love friends and, when grown, to respect wives, to be affectionate toward children, to be considerate of servants, to bear prosperity with restraint and adversity with poise, to enjoy pleasures without becoming dissolute, and to be angry without indulging in violence.[1]

In this atmosphere it is not surprising that Christians, in the course of time, were ready to claim philosophers like Socrates and Seneca as their confreres or that Christianity should have called itself the truly divine philosophy. The new religionists could ill afford to despise permanently so honorable a discipline or ignore the vast superstructure of cultural attainments that it was assumed to support.

I

On gentile soil the early Christian missionaries found themselves in the presence of a highly developed civilization, where religion had already called into its service a wide range of cultural achievements. Homer and a long line of successors among Greek and Latin poets had frequently hymned the praises of the traditional gods. The Parthenon at Athens and the Pantheon at Rome were representative products of the skill with which successive generations of heathen builders had dedicated themselves and their possessions to the gods of their faith. Every city was richly adorned with monuments of religious art. For centuries poets and architects, sculptors and

---

[1] On the praise of philosophy see Cicero *Tusculan* v. 2; Lucretius *Nature of Things* ii. 7 ff.; Epictetus *Discourses* i. 15; ii. 11; Marcus Aurelius *Meditations* ii. 17; Seneca *Epistles* lxxxix. 6; *Natural Questions, Prologue* i; Plutarch *On Educating Children* x (7E).

painters, and men of lesser genius had brought the richest offerings of their culture to the shrines of their gods.

There was a relatively large reading public within the Roman Empire at the beginning of the Christian Era. Although the printer's art was as yet unknown, publishers did a successful business in copying manuscripts by hand and placing them on sale in many cities. While classics like Homer and Vergil were always in demand, good books by more recent authors found a ready market. Perhaps the literary judgments of men at Rome in the early days of the Empire were less keen than they had been at Athens in the age of Pericles; nevertheless, Roman society in its own way had a very high appreciation of literature. Men liked good writing in prose and verse, and they had been taught by long-established custom to expect more or less lengthy treatments of religious themes in both the new and the old books that came to their hands. The religions of the Roman Empire were happy in calling into their service a poet like Vergil or a novelist like Apuleius.

Antiquity was rich also in aesthetic satisfactions for the eye. To the present day the fragmentary remains of an ancient temple, or the torso of a Greek divinity, elicits the admiration of every lover of art. But to one living in Athens, Rome, Alexandria, or Ephesus in the first century of the present era, these artistic objects were a part of the daily environment. The day-by-day living of the average citizen was relieved of its monotony by many a pageant on festival days or even by more ordinary ceremonies celebrated in connection with worship at one or another shrine. The imposing ritual, the gorgeous robes of the priests, the gaiety of the festival procession—all were an impressive sight for the people of that time. It might be the occasion of the Adonis feast at Alexandria, when people dressed in their best assembled at the temple to hear some famous soprano render a new song that Theocritus had written in honor of the god. Or at Athens one might join the procession to Eleusis to participate in the pageantry of a Demeter initiation. Perhaps at Rome it was a wild band of devotees celebrating the rites of the Phrygian goddess Cybele that occupied the center of the picture. Everywhere religion had learned to avail itself of the aesthetic values attaching to gorgeous robes, an elaborate ritual, and other displays provocative of emotion through an artistic appeal to the eye.

Roman culture presented also an appeal to the ear. The beauty of the spoken word was even more widely in demand than the charm of the written page. During the first three centuries of the present era the sophist held an eminent place in the cultural life of the Mediterranean world. He was a universally admired public entertainer, a master-performer in rhetorical declamation, who might reside permanently in the city of his choice or might move about from place to place delivering his inexhaustible torrent of words on every variety of theme. The public admired him for his readiness of speech, for the breadth of his allusions, and for what was commonly believed to be the encyclopedic character of his knowledge. His words were mighty even though his ideas might often be wholly trivial.

Heathen society was not lacking, however, in preachers of a more serious temper. There was an austere simplicity, yet a very real charm, in the discourse of the Cynic-Stoic missionary. He declared himself to be a messenger from Zeus sent to men to instruct them about good and evil. It was his mission to warn them of the wrong way and to lead them back on the right path. He spurned the rhetorician for seeking praise from his audience and affirmed that, unless the discourse of the preacher made his hearers seriously minded with reference to the problems of existence and conduct, both the message and the speaker himself were void of vitality. He used to say to his audiences: "If you have time to praise me, I speak to no purpose." When departing from his lecture hall, his hearers should be so concerned to correct their faults and abandon their errors that they would forget to congratulate the lecturer.

In imperial times much attention was devoted to the cultivation of the mind. The education of the youth was an important matter. There were many elementary schools in which boys received instruction, and the municipalities supported public schools of higher grade that in a way corresponded to the modern high school and college. There were also great universities, like those at Athens, Tarsus, and Alexandria. Then, too, there was the private school of the philosophical teacher who attracted pupils to his lectures, in which, year after year, he expounded the secrets of his particular way of thinking. These educators were Epicureans, Stoics, Platonists, or men learned in the tenets of different schools, for whom, as Epictetus says, young men left their parents, their friends, their relatives, and their estates.

The supreme achievement of the ancient mind was to be seen in this philosophical quest. By careful observation of phenomena and rigidly logical deductions, successive generations of Greek and Roman thinkers had endeavored to comprehend the true nature of the world in which they lived and to solve various speculative problems that inevitably suggested themselves to the inquiring mind. The operations of the disciplined intellect were brought to bear on questions regarding the nature of both God and man, and every educated person sought to systematize his knowledge according to the manner of thinking prevalent in one or another of the different philosophical schools. While all philosophers did not agree in their answers to the various questions that one might propound, there was general agreement among people of culture that all problems should be answered in the philosophical way. Knowledge was to be acquired and justified by the activities of the mind, and conclusions were to be deduced in accordance with men's intelligence and reason. Intellectualism was conceded to be the crowning achievement of the cultural quest among the Greeks and the Romans.

II

The Christian movement at the outset was singularly free from the leaven of Greco-Roman culture. Even when it spread beyond Palestine, it continued for several decades to retain its noncultural character. Indeed, its advocates sometimes made this fact an occasion for boasting. The lack of human wisdom in early Christianity was thought to make all the more evident its divine origin and power. The first Christians coveted none of the cultural achievements of their heathen neighbors, but, as the years passed, they learned to appropriate and claim as their own a wide range of gentile antecedents.

Primitive Christians owned no buildings devoted to the services of religion, and apparently they felt no need for such equipment. They might assemble at any place found convenient, either out-of-doors, or at the home of one of their members, or in a public hall hired for the purpose when the community became sufficiently prosperous to justify the necessary expenditure. But the building of a church edifice that would be a monument of beauty was no part of their original inclination. To employ for religious purposes ornamentation in painting and sculpture would have seemed to them improper, if not revolting. But within a few decades they learned to draw crude pictures on the walls of their catacombs, to build churches that rivaled in beauty the heathen temples, and to adorn these structures with a great wealth of symbolism in carving, painting, and sculpture.

In respect to literature it might seem that Christianity at the start was better prepared to meet gentile culture on its own ground. The sacred Scripture of the Hebrews, already translated into the Greek language for use among the Jews of the Dispersion, was held to be also a properly Christian book. But how crude it seemed to a Gentile who had even moderate literary tastes! And in fairness to Christianity it ought at once to be said that its advocates claimed for the book no eminent literary merits. Rather, they stressed its authority as revelation. For Christians it was a divine, not a human, document and, consequently, was not to be measured by currently accepted literary standards. But before many years had elapsed Christian authors appeared who strove to emulate the example of the great literary men of the Greek and Roman world. While deploring the mythological content of the ancient heathen literature, Christian writers sometimes admired and success-fully copied its stylistic qualities.

In the early days of the missionary endeavor Christianity had no substitute to offer its converts for the rich pageantry of many gentile cults. One has only to observe the conduct of those worshiping Christian assemblies described in the twelfth and fourteenth chapters of Paul's first letter to the Corinthians to perceive the relative poverty of the early Christian liturgy. The society had no ministering officials garbed in priestly robes, no impressive formalities of worship, and no elaborate ritual. Prophets spoke as the Spirit moved them, but there was little place for the delivery of a formal sermon. Some of the hymns, and perhaps even the music, were composed on the spot, and the whole performance was conspicuously lacking in those cultural appointments that had adorned worship in connection with many of the heathen cults. But in the course of time Christians learned the art of enriching their public ceremonies. They chose professional leaders and robed them impressively. They devised an elaborate ritual and a carefully ordered litany. Ultimately they also acquired an appealing Christian pageantry which captivated the imagination even of the Gentiles.

The first Christian preachers made no pretentions at skill in rhetoric. Even among Jews they had been accounted un-schooled Galileans, conspicuous for their crudity of speech. Although Paul was an educated Jew, he virtually confessed to failure in his only recorded attempt to vie with the rhetorician on the latter's own ground. Apparently Paul had believed that his sermon on Mars Hill at Athens had been a compara-tive failure, and when he moved on to Corinth he doubted whether he had ability to preach the gospel persuasively to Greeks. But he made the venture and won disciples, not by his skill in rhetoric, but by his earnest portrayal of Christ as savior. The Corinthians had been impressed by Paul's zeal, although they were fully aware of his lack of polish in speech. When the more eloquent Apollos appeared on the scene, they greeted him with applause and had no further desire to listen to the more prosaic Paul.

The apostle Paul's fine disdain for the sophist's art was not to remain a permanent Christian attitude. As time passed, the new religion increasingly drew to itself men who had been trained in the rhetorical schools, and these converts placed their mastery of words at the service of their new faith. Christian preaching in the fourth century, as represented in the sermons of Chrysostom, Ambrose, or Augustine, displayed in no small degree the polish of the sophist's discourse. But Christian preaching, in taking on elegance of form, did not completely lose the serious character which it had in the earlier age. Later Christian preachers preserved the quality of seriousness while they learned to clothe their message with the skilful diction that had been acquired in the course of their training in the rhetorical schools.

The education of children had not engaged the serious attention of the first generation of gentile converts to Christianity. The expectation of an early end of the present world made any mechanical equipment for the preservation of culture over many years to come an unnecessary undertaking. Paul had advised the Christians at Corinth to reduce the cares of family life to a minimum and to have no anxiety about the welfare of the children. If one of the parents was a Christian, that fact was thought sufficient to insure the salvation of the child (I Cor. 7:14). The notion of recruiting the membership of the church in future years from among children who had been reared under its instruction seems never to have occurred to Paul. On the contrary, he declared that the time is shortened and the fashion of this world is passing away. The Kingdom of God was imminent, and there was no time to save men by the slow processes of cultural training.

Experience ultimately taught Christians the importance of training the children for membership in the church. The church also learned the desirability of giving to converts from heathenism preliminary instruction about Christianity before admitting them to full membership. Within less than a century after the death of Paul, Christianity had in its midst teachers who conducted private schools and delivered lectures to pupils after the manner of the philosophic lecturer familiar to the Roman world of that day. By the end of the second century an institution that might be called the first Christian college was established at Alexandria, already a noteworthy center of gentile educational activity. Before the close of the fourth century Christians had interested themselves so extensively in education that it was not unusual to find them even in the public schools of the Empire teaching the Greek and Latin classics, a privilege denied them by the emperor Julian when he sought to rehabilitate paganism.

Paul had remarked that the quest for wisdom was characteristic of the Greeks, but he deplored the futility of their search. The "foolishness" of Christian preaching was to be preferred above all the wisdom of the Greek philosophers. But here again Paul's judgment upon contemporary gentile culture was much more severe than that which his successors were to exercise. In the next century one hears loyal Christian preachers proclaiming their appreciation of Greek philosophy. In many cases they had themselves been trained in the philosophical schools before they had adopted Christianity, and the cultural values thus acquired could not be hastily cast aside. These converts continued to be philosophers and found what seemed to them genuine Christian inspiration in the study of ancient Greek worthies. Greek philosophy was believed to contain a modicum of Christian wisdom, since God had allowed his truth to foreshadow itself to the Greeks through the activities of the Logos before this had become incarnate in the earthly Jesus. Thus educated, Christians freely appropriated the technique of Greek philosophy as a properly Christian instrument.

Truly the grain of mustard seed, to which Jesus had once likened the Kingdom of God, had grown to be a gigantic plant whose spreading branches sheltered birds of widely varied plumage. A wealth of cultural features, originally characteristic of Greco-Roman society, now found welcome lodgment within the new religion. Christianity in the fourth and fifth centuries had not only become the chief repository of pagan culture but claimed this inheritance as its own peculiar possession. Its rivals were no longer permitted to rear and adorn architectural monuments to the memory of their ancient gods. The old temples fell into decay or were transformed into grand Christian churches. Christ and the apostles displaced the gods of Olympus in the devotion of sculptors and painters. The production of literature and the cultivation of rhetoric found their only encouragement within ecclesiastical circles. Education also became exclusively a Christian enterprise, and no philosopher could gain a hearing outside the pale of the church.

III

Although Christianity appropriated large areas of contemporary gentile culture, it still kept intellectualism in bondage to religion. This outcome was not a peculiarly Christian development, but its vogue was greatly accelerated by the conception of the function of education that ultimately came to prevail within Christianity. The activities of the mind had to be suppressed in the interests of an allegedly infallible ecclesiastical institution.

Christianity inherited from the past a twofold educational ideal, one Semitic in origin and the other essentially Greek. Among the Hebrews learning was the care of religion which sponsored and fostered the school and provided educators with both the materials for study and the ideals to be attained. Revelation and sacred tradition furnished specific answers to all the important questions that the inquiring mind might ask regarding the world and mankind. The answers had been rendered in early days by poets of artistic feeling, by prophets with high emotional energy, by priests devoted to the interests of their cult, and without the aid of the philosopher. Under these circumstances the teacher and the thinker were servants of traditional religion.

Among the Greeks intellectualism had a different genesis and was nourished in a different atmosphere. There religion did not at the outset assume the responsibility for education. Schools and universities were secular institutions, and the individual thinker recognized no allegiance to any authority beyond his own mental compulsion. Even ethical instruction was left mainly in the hands of the educationalists; it was not chiefly the concern of either priest or prophet. Yet one must not imagine that religious and intellectual interests among the Greeks existed in complete isolation from one another. Quite the contrary was the fact. Not only did current religion assign the Greek philosopher his chief problems, but often it assumed the right to censor his conclusions. Yet he did not recognize himself as its servant, nor was he the conspicuous spokesman of any existing religious institution. In this setting the intellectual quest of the Greek was of a quite different type from that of the Jew.

The Greek philosopher spoke as an individual and based his utterances on his personal observation of things as he saw them. His conclusions represented the results of his own mental agitation rather than the reiteration of authoritative words derived from an ancient revelation. Over against custom and tradition he set intellectual acumen and logical integrity. He sought to read the secrets of the world by observing the things about him in nature, and, when his mind ranged beyond nature into metaphysical realms, his native mental processes provided the norm for constructing the order of the world beyond. In principle he recognized no question not open to further investigation and no territory too sacred for the operation of his prying gaze. Probably one ought to add that in this process of intellectual inquiry the Greek philosopher had no desire to desecrate sanctities except when they were thought to be false and harmful. For him the very search for truth through mental activity was itself the most sacred enterprise that could engage one's attention.

Religion was so pervasive an interest in Greek society that the philosopher, whatever may have been his original purpose, early found himself on the defensive. This tension was only heightened when he applied his curiosity to the problems of religion. While today we may regard the religious beliefs of the ancient Greeks as a body of absurd mythology, for the men of Athens in Socrates' day the myths were just as really valid theology as were the pronouncements of the Nicene Council for orthodox Christians of the fourth century. More than one philosopher was to learn that the attempt to intellectualize traditional religion led out upon an exceedingly thorny pathway. Current beliefs were jealous of their rights, and they could always claim to possess the validity of tradition and to represent majority opinion. In their way the Greeks were as loyal to their religious traditions as were the Jews to theirs.

Had the intellectual ideals of the older Greek thinkers prevailed, an extensive rephrasing of current religious notions would have been necessary. But this strenuous effort of the intellect ultimately broke down even among the Greeks. Before their cultural heritage was passed on to Christianity, a more conciliatory policy of handling the problem of religion and learning in relation to each other had been generally adopted. The philosopher assumed discretion to be the better part of valor and decided to abandon direct attack on established traditions. Instead, he sought to effect an honorable compromise. The method of procedure varied from time to time, but the outcome was always the same—in the end intellect yielded to tradition.

The most influential schools of philosophy in the Roman

Empire, particularly the Stoics and the Neoplatonists, gradually succumbed to the popular demand for the preservation of tradition. By means of allegorical interpretation they found a way to transform without seeming to reject current beliefs, and they even devised a technique which made it possible for them to resort to revelation rather than to the normal operations of the mind as a means of attaining to the highest type of knowledge. While the Stoic could not take literally the stories about the gods reported in Homer and Hesiod, he soon learned how to peer behind the external form of the myth in his search for an acceptable meaning. For the man of culture there might be only one divine energy pervading and controlling the universe, yet even the scholar could use the terminology of popular polytheism, since he understood that its gods were merely convenient names for different manifestations of the one primal divine essence.

In the course of time the whole content of popular mythology was effectively allegorized. If the untutored man took the legends literally, he was not to be denied their use, but an effort was made to instruct him in the true meaning of the various stories. If, for example, it seemed incongruous to believe that a supernatural being like Hephaestus should be permanently lame, or if the story that Zeus in a moment of rage hurled Hephaestus down from Olympus was thought unworthy of a deity, Stoic teachers stood ready to extract noble truths out of this mythological imagery. The incident had not actually occurred, but the story had been told to teach a great spiritual lesson. The precipitous plunge of Hephaestus from heaven signified figuratively that men had been divinely blessed by the rays of the sun falling on the earth and by the use of fire obtained from lightning, while the lameness of the god kept before one's mind the truth that all earthly fire is inferior to its more brilliant heavenly source. Thus all the familiar labels of tradition could be retained. Intellectual effort spent itself in devising new allegorical meanings to light up the old phrases. The old skins were filled with new wine, although no doubt the exponents of the method would have stoutly affirmed that they were merely restating old truth in new language. The Neoplatonists went even beyond the Stoics in yielding to tradition and revelation at the expense of rigorous mental effort. For Plotinus, the founder of the school, the attainment of ultimate reality came as the climax of an emotion. The goal was not to be reached simply by strenuous intellectual discipline. Highest knowledge lay outside the area of the mind's activity; it was in essence a new revelation of the unknowable. Mystical experience was now far more important for philosophers than was the empirical quest for knowable facts in the world of nature and the organization of knowledge in accordance with rigid logic. The popular religious cults, with their stimulating rites, offered an easy means of inducing the revelatory emotions that men craved. The later advocates of Neoplatonism were little more than diligent apologists for the traditional pagan cults. Intellectual effort expended itself in mystical yearning and in the allegorical interpretation of ancient mythology. It was now thought to be the supreme duty of the philosopher not to question the validity of the myths but to affirm their divine character. Creative mental effort had thus been virtually eliminated from the sphere of religion, and the dominance of faith over knowledge remained unchallenged.

Ultimately among Gentiles, as among Jews, intellectualism was completely subordinated to the dogmas and institutions of religion. Ancient tradition claimed to be the final authority regarding what man should think about the great problems of life and the cosmos. It was inevitable that Christianity should inherit this prevailing custom of subordinating research to accepted opinions. In the last resort truth was accredited by supernatural revelation. Paul's thesis still held good. Since the world through its wisdom knew not God, it had been decreed that men should be saved by a revelation which the philosophers might call foolishness. But even the foolishness of God was wiser than all the wisdom of men.

After Christianity adopted an educational program, it still maintained the supremacy of revelation. The values attaching to the Old and the New Testaments made Christianity eminently the religion of a book, and the possession of a book implied a body of supernatural truth to be imparted to devotees. At first, didactic activities followed the pattern provided by Judaism. Christian learning was biblical, and it did not aim at the acquisition of new knowledge by means of independent mental effort. Its subject matter was religious tradition, that is, a body of sacred wisdom rather than what might be called natural knowledge. And it was the function of learning, first and last, to serve the interests of an established faith received on the authority of tradition.

In the second century, Christianity evolved another educational agency more specifically Greek in its origin. This was the individual Christian philosopher, who set up his school in Rome or Alexandria or some other cultural center and carried on his work of instruction quite independently of the local ecclesiastical organization. While he made large use of the Bible in support of his teaching, he also felt at liberty to cite freely from pagan poets and philosophers. He had no intention of deviating from the commonly accepted Christian faith or of denying the validity of its traditions. But sometimes he did, after the manner of the Greek philosopher, exercise no slight independence of thought in his interpretation of tradition. One might say that he had, independently of the organized church, a secular school in which, however, the instruction was primarily religious. Yet in his new institution there were latent possibilities of independent research which even he himself did not at the time fully appreciate. His was a college or university under no religious supervision except such as he and his fellow-instructors might themselves provide.

By the year 200, signs were not lacking to indicate that possibly Christianity would furnish the opportunity for free intellectual research which Judaism had never stimulated and which Gentiles had vainly tried to effect. Certainly it was true that Christianity in the third and fourth centuries could count among its representatives some of the keenest minds in the Mediterranean world. Yet within Christianity, as truly as within Judaism and paganism, intellectual initiative was always faced by the fact that religion possessed its well-established sacred tradition. With the exception of Judaism, this was even more conspicuously true of Christianity than of any other religion in the ancient world. The stories which the Christian Bible contained about how the world had been created by the Hebrew God, how he had ordered the course of human history, and how he had authorized the new religion were even more inviolable for a Christian society than were the similar stories among the Greeks for the society in which the ancient philosophers had attempted to introduce the sobering influences of the human mind into the fanciful imagery of current mythology.

Under the given conditions it is not surprising that the earliest efforts of intellectualism within Christianity should have been expended in an apologetic task. The Christian mind did not blaze new ways to truth but devoted its powers to the defense of old ways. One did not assume that true wisdom could be derived from a critical observation of the cosmos or from the severest syllogism that human skill could devise. On the contrary, wisdom was to be found by consulting a historic and ancient body of written revelation. Knowledge of God was possible only through acquaintance with the sacred book. Hence the highest consecration of one's intellectual powers consisted in devoting them, when necessary, to a defense of the validity and finality of the Christian revelation. Yet Christians were not slow to recognize the demands made upon them by their immediate cultural environment. Students of the Bible, like Stoic interpreters of Homer, strove to modernize their religious traditions by the use of allegory. For the literal meaning of Scripture they substituted figurative interpretations suited to conditions and thinking of a later age. Christian scholars like Origen lavished a vast amount of mental energy on this allegorical task.

In still another respect the intellectual quest was compelled to walk very circumspectly within its new Christian home. Christianity esteemed itself not only a historic revelation; very early in its career it declared itself to be a divine institution. But intellectualism is essentially individualistic in its genius and can thrive only where perfect liberty is accorded the scholar to pursue his research and deduce his conclusions without institutional interference. That liberty, however, was no longer available when Arius, early in the fourth century, ventured to criticize the bishop of Alexandria for holding an illogical opinion. Arius ought to have known better than to pit his judgment, scholar though he was, against that of a powerful ecclesiastical official. But what hope was there for the full development of intellectual vigor within Christianity when an ecclesiastic, without distinctly academic interests, had power to silence a devout and well-educated subordinate who had, as it were, recently emerged with honors from the leading Christian university of the day? Christianity's rapidly increasing institutionalism was incompatible with the cultivation of a free and vigorous intellectualism. Already in the fourth century the free Christian college, such as had been conducted by Origen at Caesarea and Lucian at Antioch, was doomed to give way to another type of educational institution that would be strictly under the control of the church.

Henceforth Christianity remained a thoroughgoing supernaturalism. The present world of nature and normal human experience were consistently slighted, if not indeed thoroughly despised. It was thought improper to assume that any valuable knowledge of the true God was to be discovered by acquaintance with a world that was supposed to be infested with and dominated by wicked demons. At best the thoughts of the natural man could be but vain efforts of the imagination. The opinions of the ancient philosophers, even when admired by Christian scholars, had to be redeemed from the curse of the natural world. One said that this Greek wisdom had in reality been a Christian revelation faintly disclosed by the divine Logos operating outside Hebrew territory, or else it had been pilfered from the Old Testament by demons who had taught it to Greeks in order later to embarrass the Christian missionaries.

The Greek spirit had begun to lose its more strenuous intellectual urge before Christianity appeared on the scene, but thereafter the process of decline was accelerated. Heathen philosophers turned to Christianity in considerable numbers. The new religion had the most attractive equipment then available for insuring satisfaction when one sought to supplement the acquisitions of the mind by an appeal to authoritative tradition. No pagan cult had any heritage that could rival the Christian Bible as a source of ancient revelation, and no heathen deity was served by an institution equal in power to that of the Christian church for mediating divine help to needy mortals. Equipped with these safeguards, Christianity could freely receive into full fellowship any Greek philosopher who knocked at its doors. But it was the letter rather than the spirit of the older Greek intellectualism that Christianity thus acquired.

Unquestionably such philosophy as was appropriated by the church rendered the new cause great service. It could not be without beneficial effect upon the representatives of Christianity to strive to think the thoughts and copy the mental processes that had characterized a Heraclitus, a Socrates, a Plato, or even an Epictetus or a Plotinus. To keep such company was a great mental stimulus, provided a Christian maintained his interest in defending the validity of his religious traditions, adhered to the creeds and practices of his ecclesiastical institution, and never questioned the propriety of seeking ultimate wisdom in the realm of the supernatural. If he transgressed any of these bounds, immediately he became a heretic and an outcast.

Of the mind's scientific quest, by which new and valid wisdom is acquired through observation of nature or the reading of immediate experience, the Christian philosopher who remained orthodox could have no genuine appreciation. That spirit of scientific research which had gradually developed among the Greeks until it ultimately produced an Aristotle, failed to find a home in the intellectualism of the ancient church, just as it had failed to dominate the later pagan philosophy of the imperial age. Christian scholars no longer followed Paul, who had declared all worldly wisdom to be worthless, yet they universally assumed that any knowledge acquired outside the Bible and the church was valid only in so far as it accorded strictly with historic revelation The theologians of the church never lost sight of their inherited conviction that faith should precede and transcend knowledge and that no knowledge was valid that did not agree with traditional beliefs. Since these were guaranteed by revelation, they were superior to any form of human wisdom; the supernatural mind was thought to rule supreme over the mind of man.

CHAPTER X
THE SURVIVAL OF SUPER-NATURALISM

IN LESS than four hundred years of historical development Christianity had acquired a full supernatural equipment. No area of Jewish or gentile thinking was left uninvaded. Every form of supernatural belief current in the environment was revised or transformed and supplemented to serve the purposes of the new religion. Its doctrines, its ritual practices, its ecclesiastical institution, and its claims to supremacy over all rivals were fortified by an abundant display of divine interference in human affairs. The fanciful flights of the imagination, the rational processes of the mind, and the observational activities of the senses were all subjected to the ideal of a divinely revealed truth. Otherwise they were not to be tolerated within Christianity.

The ancients knew no other way to validate religion. The world of nature was for them a narrowly restricted area of experience hemmed in by unexplored mysteries lying beyond the horizon of their physical vision or their rational comprehension. They had to rely on imagination for an acquaintance with this unknown region. They had no hundred-inch telescope with which to read the secrets of the heavens and no sensitive microscope to lay bare the mysteries of nature's vital processes. Chemical and physical laws that today are the common property of every intelligent man were then quite un-

known to the average person. Naturalism, except for Epicureans with their fanciful doctrine of atoms falling in empty
space, was a feeble instrument for use in solving the riddles of
the universe. Its vast expanse crowded in on the imagination,
and its secrets were thought to be revealed only by a hypothetical supernaturalism. Failing to understand in any normal
way the operation of nature's forces, one could only comprehend them in terms of otherworldly powers impinging from
without upon the conditions of daily life.

I

The appeal to supernaturalism was a very valuable method
for interpreting Christianity to the ancients. This mode of
thinking was not only widely current but was most highly
esteemed by ordinary people. Had Christians been unsuccessful in this area of expansion, their religion never could have
become the prevailing faith of the Roman Empire. As a means
of defending Christianity against its critics, or of presenting it
appealingly to prospective converts, the assertion of its unique
otherworldly validity was the most powerful apologetic that
could be imagined. This was the only effective technique
available for evaluating the superior significance of a religion
in a day when the world of nature was thought to be narrowly
bounded and closely overshadowed by an upper world inaccessible to men except by the eye of faith.

Since faith was confidence in that for which one hoped and
certainty regarding the unseen (Heb. 11:1), its truth had to
be supernaturally guaranteed. Natural knowledge could at
best only hint at the truth but could not comprehend its
ultimate validity. Indeed, the human mind might go far

astray if by its normal activities it sought to establish certainty without the aid of revelation. Not every Christian would go to the extreme of saying with Tertullian that one believed a religious doctrine just because it seemed absurd (*credo quia ineptum*) to the natural man, but the truth of revelation was not to be fully demonstrated within the narrow limits of rationality. One might attempt to prove a belief reasonable, but success in that effort was not the final test of accuracy. Revelation was a higher wisdom to be accepted on the authority of heaven.

In the early days Christians seem to have relied chiefly on miracle stories to demonstrate to Gentiles the supreme authority of their religion. Shortly after the middle of the first century Paul had epitomized the Christian faith in terms of belief in the lordship of Jesus on the strength of his miraculous triumph over death (Rom. 10:9). Paul believed this to be true because he was convinced that he had seen the risen Jesus in a vision. In the last resort his personal faith rested on this experience. As Paul interpreted this unique phenomenon, God had revealed his heavenly Son to this former persecutor in order to transform the latter into a missionary of the new religion. The process had been pre-eminently a supernatural occurrence.

Throughout his career Paul depended on visions and revelations for fresh knowledge to meet the exigencies of life. He shared with other Christians the ability to work miracles through the power of the risen Christ whose spiritual presence was their constant possession. To "walk by the Spirit" was to enjoy continually a supernatural guidance for belief and conduct. Among the special privileges that God had bestowed on members of the Spirit-endowed Christian community was the ability of some persons to perform miracles and to exercise gifts of healings (I Cor. 12:28). Paul so highly prized his miracle-working power that, when challenged by his enemies, he cited this equipment as the ultimate proof of his title to apostleship. Whatever prerogatives others might claim, none could excel him in his manifestly supernatural ability to perform mighty works (II Cor. 12:12). And miracles were the final test of the validity and efficiency of faith (Gal. 3:5).

In the generation after Paul, a new type of miracle story was advanced in support of Christian supernaturalism. Paul had made no mention of miracles performed by Jesus during his earthly career. It was not until after his ascent to heaven that his Spirit, operating through the medium of the disciples, demonstrated its miracle-working powers. But the author of the Gospel of Mark reported that the earthly Jesus had begun the display of this supernatural energy immediately after the Spirit had descended upon him at the time of his baptism. And subsequently, when Matthew and Luke were written, the physical birth of Jesus had become the initial miraculous event that marked the inception of Christian supernaturalism.

Another line of argument was developed on the basis of the divine authority of the Hebrew Scriptures. Jesus, it was said, had fulfilled predictions made by the ancient prophets, thus giving to Christianity all the supernatural rights claimed by the Jews for their ancestral religion. God had designed from the beginning that Christianity should be the climactic manifestation of the total process of revelation. Jesus had been a second and a superior Moses. The new teachings set forth by Jesus and promulgated by Christians supplemented and transcended those of the older regime and carried forward to complete fulfilment the purposes of God in creating the world and in guiding the Hebrews throughout their history. They had been the unique miracle-race, but they were now supplanted by Christians who possessed in a heightened degree all the supernatural credentials belonging to the ancients.

By the close of the second century the scriptural authentication of Christianity had been enlarged to include a group of early Christian writings to supplement the Jewish Old Testament. These new books, since they were accepted as an additional body of revelation, now became a further source of support for belief in the supernatural. They were divinely inspired documents that had to be accepted on faith. Henceforth contact with the supernatural was mediated by the written page rather than by spontaneous response to guidance by the Holy Spirit or assent to the evidence of miracles. The evidential value of an experiential fact was replaced by a formal dogma affirmed on scriptural authority and so to be explicitly accepted by an unquestioning faith.

When gentile philosophers—such men as Justin Martyr and Clement of Alexandria—accepted Christianity, more consideration was given to the question of the rational justification of faith. But by that date the supremacy of tradition had become so firmly established that the essential beliefs of Christianity were immune from any rational criticism. One first believed and afterward exercised his mental powers to defend or expound and enlarge the content of his faith. Christian truth was a body of divinely revealed wisdom superior to all proof, as Justin affirmed. When items of Greek wisdom seemed too valuable to be discarded, they were endowed with supernatural validity by ascribing them to the shadowy activities of the divine Logos in the gentile world at large prior to the rise of Christianity.

The natural world was more highly esteemed by Clement of Alexandria than by most of his Christian contemporaries. This was his inheritance from Stoicism. But this did not mean for Clement any disposition to question the supremacy of supernaturalism. Ultimate Christian truth was still a matter of special revelation, but one who read nature aright could see everywhere in it evidence of God's overruling wisdom and goodness. Therefore, it was a valuable source of knowledge to supplement the unique revelation disclosed in the Scriptures and in Christian tradition. Thus supernaturalism remained supreme while nature constituted a dependable source of information to clarify and supplement Christian faith. Every true Christian started with simple faith, which he never doubted or abandoned, but confirmed and magnified by the addition of natural knowledge to be acquired by the skill of the Christian philosopher.

Origen pursued with zeal the philosophical quest, but he esteemed natural knowledge less highly than did Clement. This was a consequence of Origen's preference for Platonism over Stoicism. Plato's dual world—the world of spirit which is totally incorporeal and the lower world of matter—assigned nature to an inferior level of existence and elevated supernaturalism to a position of new dignity. Since it came ultimately from the spirit world it had to be divinely revealed, and Origen held this revelation to be available only in the Scriptures and in the traditions of Christianity. Neither philosophical speculation nor logic, but only the divine wisdom which reached its consummation in Christ, was a dependable source of Christian truth. Hence philosophy, the study of which Origen industriously cultivated, did not yield new truth but was an apologetic instrument for defending the validity of supernatural revelation.

Henceforth Christian thinkers paid less and less attention to the natural world as a source of religious knowledge. Not to understand the world of nature but ultimately to escape from it by means of a divinely revealed program of redemption became the dominant concern. Early in the fourth century Arnobius had specifically condemned the exercise of any curiosity regarding natural phenomena that might detract attention from the all-important matter of the salvation of the soul. Similarly Augustine, a century later, deprecated any interest in natural science, since all that one needed to know about the physical universe had been authoritatively recorded in the Scriptures. Under the influence of Neoplatonism, interest in the ideal world of spiritual reality had quite smothered out curiosity regarding the natural order, and men's minds turned to speculation about the unseen universe. This tendency strengthened the vogue of Christian supernaturalism which continued to hold its position practically unassailed for several centuries.

II

By the beginning of the twelfth century the rights of reason as a guide to Christian thinking began to be revived. At first the motive was the defense rather than the criticism of tradition, but even to admit the need and the propriety of defending Christian belief by human reason, apart from the compulsion of revelation, meant a virtual infringement upon the prerogatives of the supernatural.

When Anselm proposed to defend certain prevalent Christian beliefs on purely rational grounds, he had no intention of discounting the full authority of revelation. He still adhered to Augustine's affirmation that we first believe in order that we may have true knowledge. But Anselm thought it possible to prove by rational processes the validity of Christian doctrine even if one did not already possess basic Christian faith. This he undertook to accomplish in some of his best-known writings, and thereby he set the pattern for a type of Christian apologetic that endowed the human mind with a capacity for arriving at truth without the aid of revelation. This procedure did not deliberately aim at invalidating supernaturalism, but its tendency was to make man's mind a dependable guide in the acquisition of religious truth. It was still a long time before the logical outcome of Anselm's position came to definite expression. If consistently pursued, it would have surrendered the supernatural accreditation of dogma in favor of the plain test of rationality.

Abelard faced the same problem as did Anselm and took a further step toward its solution. Although he never affirmed that no Christian doctrine should be believed until it was rationally understood, he did hold that no manifestly irrational belief was to be accepted. He adhered faithfully to the notion of a divinely inspired Bible, but he refused to ascribe a similar validity to the later forms of Christian tradition even when they were supported by the testimony of the early Church Fathers. He still maintained that faith was basic for all religious knowledge, but one who believed too quickly without first understanding the truth was "light-minded." He would not concede, as some of his predecessors had affirmed, that faith is without merit if it is supported by human reason. This was equivalent to saying that any allegedly supernatural revelation that contradicts reason is to be rejected. But, in requiring faith to be rational, Abelard had no thought of denying the validity of revealed truth. This was still the foundation of all Christian wisdom.

No medieval Christian thinker struggled more heroically with the problem of the natural and the supernatural than did Thomas Aquinas. He had come under the influence of Aristotle, who taught him to regard nature much more highly than had been the custom within Christianity since the days of Clement of Alexandria. The latter had the Stoic's respect for nature as the very embodiment of rational deity, while Aristotle's god was merely the "prime mover" who was not intimately involved in concrete natural events. And Aristotle assumed that all human knowledge was derived only from perception by the physical senses. Hence it was never an affair of special divine revelation. If Thomas had followed Aristotle consistently, he would have had to reject outright the traditional Christian view of the primacy of faith, but this he refused to do. At the same time he adopted the Aristotelian dictum that sense experience is the source of all human knowledge. He spent his life trying to harmonize this Aristotelian epistemology with traditional Christian faith in the supernatural.

The outcome of Thomas' efforts was the famous doctrine of two complementary types of Christian thinking known as natural theology and revealed theology. In elaborating the former type, Thomas dignified nature as a source of sense perception by which the rational individual could rise to a true knowledge of God without recourse to revelation. In this way one might "ascend through created things to the knowledge of God." But there was also a revealed truth that was wholly inaccessible to natural reason. This was the content of faith which "descends by way of revelation from God to us." According to Thomas, Christianity rightfully embodied both techniques, which were supplementary but never contradictory. Thus Christianity in the higher reaches of truth was a genuine supernaturalism, although in a large measure its truth could be attained by the natural reason of man. One recognized "the light of natural reason" and "the light of divine revelation," but never permitted any deviation of the former from the latter. Supernaturalism was still supreme, although considerably sobered by its association with nature and human reason.

III

The rights of human reason and the testimony of the natural order now became the two chief antagonists with which supernaturalism had to contend. Ultimately the views of Thomas Aquinas became the accepted standard of thinking for Roman Catholicism, while the various Protestant bodies reverted to the traditional faith of primitive Christianity. But in the seventeenth century the movement known as rationalism awakened once more lively debate on the subject. The leading rationalists made human reason the primary norm for measuring the validity of religious truth. While they did not reject belief in the supernatural, they assigned it a role of secondary importance and insisted that it was to be rationally justified. Rational religion was enough for the intelligent person, but revelation had been added as a means of establishing religious duties and promoting virtue. Yet the operations of revelation were thought to be in strict harmony with the findings of natural religion. One accepted supernaturalism in so far as its testimony was capable of rational defense.

In the extremer form of deism, belief in the supernatural was practically ignored. Since it served for the rationalists merely to bolster virtue, it was not needed by the Deists, because they believed that everything contributing to virtue could be known most accurately by reason. The moral perfection of God could be most adequately perceived by rational processes of thought, and the goal of all worthy religion was man's apprehension and imitation of God's virtues in the interests of both individual and public good. Arguments from prophecy and miracle seemed unworthy of an enlightened mind and liable to be a detriment rather than an advantage to the most valuable type of morality, in which for these thinkers religion principally consisted.

The German philosopher Kant struck an even heavier blow against traditional supernaturalism by adding to rationalistic thinking a stronger emphasis on moralism. He did not reject the notion that Christianity was both a revealed and a natural religion, but he maintained that it had no need of prophecy and miracles to enforce its moral precepts. To assume that God required of man anything beyond right living was mere superstition; it was absurd to imagine that an allegedly revealed truth had a validity transcending human intelligence. The mind of man was so constituted that it was capable of comprehending the full content of religious truth.

Thus spiritual values became an integral part of the natural order, and supernaturalism virtually faded out of the picture. Reason and conscience in the enlightened individual increasingly asserted their rights over the divine authority of a traditional revelation.

In the meantime a greatly enlarged view of the natural world had been taking shape. The astronomical researches of Copernicus, Galileo, and Kepler had brought the heavenly bodies within the range of man's mental comprehension. Francis Bacon's new method of investigating nature and the mathematical physics of Isaac Newton vastly extended man's understanding of his universe even in the seventeenth century. In subsequent years the scientific quest continued to gather momentum until today the world of nature has become a limitless area over which the mind of man ranges freely in its search for the secrets of the orderly cosmos. The knowable processes of nature have become so extensive in their range and so wide in their scope that no room is left for such arbitrary intervention of supernatural forces as was possible in the mysterious little world in which the early Christians lived.

The present-day outcome for belief in supernaturalism is threefold. The ancient mode of thinking which has been passed down in Christian tradition is still widely represented by persons who have given little or no heed to modern knowledge of nature. The biblical imagery of divine intervention regardless of physical laws is uncritically perpetuated by religious people who pray to God to change the weather or to alter some other natural course of events in order to show some special material favors to the suppliant. At the other extreme are those who so magnify the physical reality of the universe that the material facts of life are self-controlled and leave no room for any operation of spiritual forces inherent in the making of history or in individual experience.

A third form of thinking rejects the traditional brand of supernatural imagery, which depicts divine action as an arbitrary interference with nature by an otherworldly power, but seeks within the natural world itself evidence of the spiritual strivings and ideal values that belong in the sphere of religion. These are the religious naturalists, whom their opponents are wont to call strict materialists but who stoutly repudiate the accusation. They find in history and in the normal processes of human living evidences of a spiritual reality that seems to them more tolerable, trustworthy, and significant than anything propounded by the traditional type of belief in revelation handed down from a transcendental realm.

The prominence given to supernaturalism by the early interpreters of Christianity readily leads many persons to the conclusion that this way of thinking was the essential item in the new religion. In that event to refuse to believe in the original form of Christian supernaturalism as represented by its early interpreters would seem to place one outside of genuine Christianity. But if religion is more ultimately an experiential way of life that may be subjected to varying interpretations according to current ways of thinking regarded as valid at different times and by different people, then interpretations become only variant ways of evaluating the ideals and attainments of religious living.

The incentives for pursuing certain ideals or exemplifying specific attitudes may be regarded by one person as supernaturally imposed obligations dictated from above out of the transcendental sphere. Or they may be called by another person normal acquisitions of the human spirit in communion with the vital forces of nature that are expressive of the divine will. In the one instance God is sought in the remote regions beyond the natural order, while in the other instance his presence is most clearly manifest in the operations of natural law, in the emergence of social ideals, in the upsurgence of human morality, and in the spiritual outreach of religious living. It is the quality of the life that determines its significance, regardless of whether it is given a natural or a supernatural interpretation.

This distinction applies to Christianity even during those early days when it was elaborating its abundant supernaturalism. When Paul interpreted his experience as a miraculous endowment by the Holy Spirit enabling him to work wonders, it did not mean that everyone had to adopt the same view in order to be a Christian. The more fundamental requirement was a specific type of life to be exemplified by every member of the new society. In almost every Pauline letter nearly half the space was given up to practical admonitions regarding the ideals one should cherish and practice. To speak with tongues was thought by the Corinthians—and by Paul—to be a distinctly supernatural endowment, yet the practice of love in one's daily conduct was much more essential to a genuine Christianity. The character of the ideals that dominated one's life was the fundamental matter in religion, but the type of interpretation that one adopted to give theoretical validity to the ideals was a variable quantity subject to personal tastes and current ways of thinking.

Christian supernaturalism arose to serve a functional need

in the course of the new religion's expansion within its particular environment and in relation to characteristic modes of thinking prevalent in that day. As such it rendered valuable service in advancing the cause of religion as represented in the lives of Christian believers. But their type of life was more fundamentally important than the form of theoretical justification adopted to support its validity. As time passed, the hypothetical apologetic altered because it lost its convincing quality for future generations. Spiritual and moral ideals continued to be exemplified in living persons, who no longer recognized the virtue of the earlier arguments that had been advanced to give them validity. To maintain rigid adhesion to an outworn type of interpretation might prove in reality detrimental to Christianity in a day when newer forms of thinking had become more efficient in supporting the ideals and aims of Christian living in a modern world.

INDEX

Abaddon, 25
Abelard, 227–28
Abraham, 3–4, 23, 91
Achilles, 28, 71, 181
Adonis, 81–82
Aeneas, 29, 85
Aeschylus, 106
Aesculapius; *see* Asklepios
Agabus, 61
Agamemnon, 71
Augustus, 85, 124, 126–28
Alcmene, 87
Alexander the Great, 76, 88, 122, 131, 162; apparitions of, 37, 72
Allegory, 212–13, 216
Ambrose, 206
Ananias, 17
Angels: in Christian thinking, 68; Philo's doctrine of, 67
Anselm, 227
Anthropomorphism, polemic against, 36
Aphrodite, 81
Apocalypse of Peter, 195
Apollo, 54, 77, 88–90, 112, 130, 158, 160
Apollos, 206
Apologetics, 216
Apparitions: of Alexander the Great, 37; Christian belief in, 22 ff.; Epicurean denial of, 31; gentile belief in, 28 ff.; of the heavenly Christ, 34; Jewish belief in, 23 ff.; of Patroclus, 28; Platonic view of, 31; of Romulus, 38; skepticism about, 31; Stoic view of, 31
Appian, 74
Apuleius, 66, 103, 165, 167–68, 200

Aratus, 9
Archagathus, 154
Aristotle, 71, 100, 174, 219, 228
Arius, 217
Arnobius, 226
Arrian, 131
Artemis, 115
Arval Brothers, 114
Asa, 155
Ascension, of Caesar, 48
Ashur, 129
Asklepios, 77, 88, 154, 158, 160–61
Athena, 131
Athenodorus, 33, 111
Atticus, 38
Attis, 82
Augur, function of, 45
Augustine, 182, 206, 226–27
Augustus, 53, 74–75, 89, 109, 122, 134, 144
Aulus Gellius, 108

Bacchus, 80, 114
Bacis, a prophet, 57
Bacon, Francis, 231
Baptism, 20
Barnabas, 18, 35
Bible, of Christians, 54

Caligula, 183
Caracalla, 66
Castor, 39, 87
Celsus, 128
Chemosh, 129
Children, 207
Chrysostom, 206

235

PRINTED IN U·S·A